MANAGING RESIDENTIAL PROPERTY

DAVID WATSON

EMERALD PUBLISHING

Emerald Guides
Brighton BN7 2SH

© Straightforward Publishing 2012

978184716162298

Printed by Berforts Press

Cover design by Bookworks Islington

Contents

The Property Investors Management Handbook

Introduction

INTRODUCTION

Letting property

This revised edition of The Property Investors Management Handbook has been expanded to cover buying property during a recession. Its aim is to demonstrate in a clear and uncomplicated way the key elements in buying and managing residential property. In the main the book is intended for the investor but can also be used by those who wish to gain a background in property management generally.

Although it is harder for the would be landlord to gain access to the buy-to-let sector at this point in time, the opportunities for landlords to invest and make a decent return are better than ever, with rents across Britain set to rise by more than 20% over the next five years and more and more individuals and families moving into the private rented sector. Overall, private letting of residential property has grown significantly in the last 25 years, particularly with the passage of the 1988 Housing Act which gave landlords more incentive to let. However, in some cases those who are involved in letting property do not have the professional knowledge needed to manage effectively and often end up in a mess. Little thought is given to the fact that a complex framework of law, which both parties should recognise, covers the landlord and tenant, defining the relationship between the two.

Whilst the public sector has taken great pains to educate the landlord and tenant, the private sector has not followed suit. This book should, hopefully remedy some of those shortcomings and make the process of managing property for a profit that much easier.

Generally the key to understanding any situation is having knowledge of a particular subject. The law and business environment relating to housing is one very important area.

This Guide is intended to provide clear answers for the landlord, existing or potential by outlining the business and legal environment and also rights and obligations in general and by pointing to the way forward in a particular situation. The book covers the acquisition, letting and managing of property in depth and should enable the landlord, or potential landlord to manage effectively and efficiently, at the same time protecting his or her asset.

Also included in this revised edition is an updated detailed guide to landlord tax obligations, including capital gains tax and advice on how to minimize liability.

The guide should also be of use to the student who wants a brief introduction to the law relating to private residential lettings.

This book is essential reading for any landlord or potential landlord and should prove to be invaluable.

David Watson

1

CONSIDERATIONS WHEN RENTING OUT A PROPERTY

....

Investing in Property During a Recession

Demand for property investment has remained strong during this current recession, indeed, the overall demand for private rented property is stronger than ever, with the mortgage market restricted for purchasers and house price inflation, particularly in the south east, creating the need for high deposits which people cannot find. Lending has become far more stringent, owing to the onset of the credit crunch and the banks unwillingness to loan money, particularly to property investors. Essentially, accessing finance has become a big issue. The banks favor those with large cash deposits. This is the same in the buy-to-let sector as for domestic mortgages.

However, if finance can be arranged then the yields that one can expect from buy-to-let properties are high by comparison, currently standing at 6%. A yield is a portfolio's annual rental income as a percentage of total value. The reason is that demand for private rented property is high, particularly as first time buyers cannot get a toehold in the market. They are instead turning to the private rental sector. Therefore, investing in property, for the longer term, as opposed to investing for short-term gain, is still a viable option.

As with everything, property is a good investment as long as it is managed well. Too many landlords (so called landlords) buy property and neglect it which has a negative impact on the environment and also a negative impact on the investment as a whole. A run down property will decrease in value and the possibility of renting it out for a full market rent will also diminish.

That is what this book is all about-how to become a good landlord and a good property manager and how to maximize the returns on your property.

The importance of having a clear business plan

Letting residential property for profit has become more and more common in the last twenty years, particularly since the passage of the 1988 Housing Act, which gave potential landlords more incentive to let by removing rent controls for property let after 1988 and also changing the tenancy in use to the assured tenancy, a version of which is the assured shorthold, fixed for a minimum period of six months and easily ended after that period.

Added to the passage of the 1988 Act has been the activities of the housing market which boomed in the eighties and then predictably went bust, boomed again in the nineties and then went bust and then boomed again. Right now, we are in the middle of the worst downturn for many years and the importance of clear advice to landlords is more crucial than ever.

In addition to the many who let property out of necessity and who are not "professional landlords" so to speak there are those who have built a business through acquiring properties, mostly through mortgage and letting them out for a profit. These professional landlords differ as to their expertise, some being very unprofessional in their approach, having no real idea of Landlord and Tenant law and no idea of the property world and subsequently very little idea of management. Often these people come unstuck and cause grief to others, whether intentionally or otherwise.

The aim of this section is to introduce the landlord, whether potential or already involved in the business, to the key aspects of the world of residential letting in the hope that that person becomes more knowledgeable and that profit is maximized whilst management is effective and equitable.

What kind of property is suitable for letting?

Obviously there are a number of different markets when it comes to people who rent. There are those who are less affluent, young and single, in need of a sharing situation, but more likely to require more intensive management than older more mature (perhaps professional) people who can afford a higher rent but require more for their money. The type of property you have, its location, its condition, will very much determine the rent levels that you can charge and the clients that you will attract.

The type of rent that a landlord might expect to achieve will be around ten per cent of the value of the freehold of the property, (or long leasehold in the case of flats). The eventual profit will be determined by the level of any existing mortgage and other outgoings.

If you are renting a flat it could be that it is in a mansion block or other flatted block and the service charge will need to be added to the rent. When letting a property for a profit it is necessary to consider profit after mortgage payments and likely tax bill plus other outgoings such as insurance and agents fees (if any). Of course there are other factors which make the profit achieved less important, that is the capital growth of the property. See further on in the book for a breakdown of taxation and allowances.

The business plan

As a (would be) private landlord, a person considering letting a property for profit, or already doing so, it is vital that you are very clear about the following:

- What kind of approach do you intend to take as a landlord? Do you intend to purchase, or do you have, an up market property which you are going to rent out to stable professional tenants who will pay their rent on time and look after the property (hopefully!).
- What are the key factors that affect the value of a property in rental terms? Is the property close to public transport, does it have a garden, what floor is it on and what size are the rooms? Is it secure and in a crime free area? If you are acquiring a property you should set out what it is you are trying to achieve in the longer term, i.e. the type of person you want and match this to the likely residential requirements of that hypothetical person. You can then gain an idea of what type of property you are looking for, in what area, and you can then see whether or not you can afford such a property. If not, you may have to change your plan.
- Do you intend to let to young single people, perhaps students, who will occupy individual rooms achieving higher returns but causing potentially greater headaches? Are you aware of the headaches? It is vitally important that you understand the ramifications of letting to different client groups and the potential problems in the future.
- Are you clear about the impact on the environment, and to other people, that your activities as a landlord may have? For example, do

14

you have a maintenance plan which ensures that not only does your property look nice and remain well maintained but also takes into account whether the plan, or lack of it, will have an impact on the rest of the neighborhood? Will the type of tenant you intend to attract affect the rest of those living in the immediate vicinity

- What are the aims and objectives underpinning your business plan? Do you have a business plan or are you operating in an unstructured way? Taking into account the above, it is obviously necessary that you have a clear picture of the business environment that you intend to operate in, the legal and economic framework that governs and regulates the environment.
- It is vital that you are very clear about what it is you are trying to achieve. You should either understand the type of property that you already own or have an idea of the property you are trying to acquire to fit what client group. These goals should be very clear in your own mind and based on a long-term projection, underpinned by knowledge of the law and economics of letting property.
- As an exercise you should sit down and map out your business plan, before you go any further. Whether you are an existing property owner, or wish to acquire a property for the purpose of letting, the first objective is to formulate a business plan.

Now read the main points from chapter one.

Main points from chapter one

- Letting residential property for investment has become more and more common over the last ten years.
- Although there has been a downturn in the market, property is still seen as a good long-term investment. The demand for private rented property is set to increase along with an increase in rents.
- There are a number of different markets when it comes to people who rent. The markets are defined mainly by economic factors.
- The type of rent a landlord will expect will vary and the profit will be determined by size of mortgage in relation to rent and also by other outgoings on the property.
- It is vital that a landlord, or prospective landlord has a business plan that sets out aims and objectives of investment.
- It is vital that you are clear about what you are trying to achieve.

2

BUYING A HOUSE OR FLAT FOR INVESTMENT

....

Budget

Before beginning to look for a house or flat for investment you need to sit down and give careful thought to the costs.

Deposit

Sometimes the estate agent will ask you for a small deposit when you make the offer. This indicates that you are serious about the offer and is a widespread and legitimate practice, as long as the deposit is not too much. £100 is usual.

The main deposit for the property, i.e. the difference between the mortgage and what has been accepted for the property, isn't paid until the exchange of contracts. Once you have exchanged contracts on a property the purchase is legally binding. Until then, you are free to withdraw. The deposit cannot be reclaimed after exchange.

Banks will normally lend up to 85 percent of the purchase price of the property for buy to let. However, the less you borrow the more favorable terms you can normally get from a bank or building society. This particularly applies now, with the onset of the credit-crunch and a tightening up of lending criteria.

Mortgages

Buy-to-let mortgages are slowly becoming more attainable, after a period of retrenchment in the market as a whole, arising because of the banks desire to be cautious in their policies of lending. There is competition now, with Buy-to-let specialist lender Paragon once again becoming active. Typically, a person raising a buy to let mortgage will need to find between 25-35% deposit depending on the lender and the deal. First time investors typically need to own their own property to get into the market and also have to demonstrate income of at least £25,000 per year. Lenders also require rents to equal 125% of mortgage payments on a buy-to-let property. For example, a £500 monthly mortgage repayment would have to achieve rent of at least £625 a month.

Building a portfolio

Those who already own buy-to-let properties and are looking to expand for the first time since the credit crunch face further hurdles given the lack of finance. It is, however, still very possible to expand a portfolio with several building societies Most mortgage providers allow each investor to have up to 10 properties with a maximum of three mortgaged with that particular lender. It is a case of shopping around for the best deal.

If you are a professional landlord who wants to invest in a larger range of properties you will need to go to a specialist lender. Two such specialist lenders are Shawbrook bank, a recently formed bank and paragon. they have deals for larger landlords, or those that want to expand, including those with Houses in Multi-Occupation (HMO's).

18

Stamp duty

Although there are several dodges which allow property owners to avoid stamp duty, most people have to pay this. Stamp duty is a tax paid on property-zero for properties costing up to £125,000 (£250,000 for first time buyers, although this is set to change back from 24th March 2012) 1% of purchase price between £125,001 to £250,000-3% from £250,001 to £500,000-4% £500,001 to 1m and 5% over 1m.

Energy Performance Certificates (EPC's)

EPC's are compulsory for all rental homes (from 1st October 2008). Therefore all landlords are required to commission an EPC.

As seen above, an EPC surveyor will assess the property and looks at all the ways a house or flat can waste heat, such as inadequate loft insulation, lack of cavity wall insulation, draughts and obsolete boilers. After the assessment they will award a rating from A (as good as it gets) to G (terrible). The document also includes information and advice on how to improve matters, such as lagging the water tank or installing double-glazing. An EPC costs between £120-130 (although shop around and you can get them cheaply or for nothing at all (as part of estate agents inducements) and is valid for ten years. Improvements made while the certificate is in force will not need a new survey.

Examples

There are three examples presented below which will enable the potential investor to get an idea of what problems might be inherent in a range of properties. Obviously, these are three isolated examples but you will get an idea of what to expect.

Example 1.
The city-centre Flat
Type of house: A two-bedroom flat, built in 1993.
Location: the Jewellery Quarter Birmingham.

Current energy efficient rating: 80% (C)

Potential energy efficiency rating:

82% (B)

Current bills: £198 per year

Potential savings per year: £13

Main failings: Manually controlled heating.

Proposed improvements typically costing less than £500. None

Proposed improvements typically costing more than £500. Install automatically controlled fan-assisted storage heaters, at a cost of about £1,000 for a property of this size (saving £13 per year)

The Georgian Farmhouse

Type of house: Five-bedroom farmhouse, built around 1800.

Location: Ratlinghope near Shrewsbury Shropshire.

Current energy efficiency rating: 30% (F)

Potential energy efficiency rating: 48% (E)

Potential savings: £550 per year.

Main failings: Solid stone walls are not good insulators, the main floor is built directly onto the earth, leaking heat. Only 20% of the windows are double glazed. There is only one energy efficient light bulb.

Proposed improvements costing less than £500. Add 2inches of insulation to the stone walls, at a cost of about £40m square (saving £470 per year) top up loft insulation to 250mm, costing about £240 (saving £58 per year) install low energy lighting (saving £15 per year).

Proposed improvements typically costing £500 or more. Change all windows to double glazing, costing about £350 per window (saving £39 per year) install photovoltaic cells-a typical domestic system costs between £10,000 and £18,000 to install, saving £68 per year.

The London terrace

Type of house: A four-bedroom terraced house built in 1912.

Location: Wandsworth, south London.
Current energy efficient rating: 56% (D).
Current bills: £952 per year.
Potential energy efficient rating: 56% (D).
Potential savings: £247 per year.

Main failings: Solid brick walls without insulation; suspended timber floor; no low-energy lighting; no individually controllable radiators;

only 55% double glazing; non-condensing gas boiler.

Proposed improvements typically costing less than £500. Add 2inches of insulation to solid walls, at a cost of about £40 per m2 (saving £170 per year); top up loft insulation by 250mm-cost £240, saving £30 per year; add insulation to hot water tank and pipe-work costing about £300, saving about £19 per year.

Proposed improvements typically costing more than £500 per year. Install thermostatic radiator valves, which cost £250-£300 per radiator saving about £39 per year. Further improvements could be made installing solar water heating-a domestic system will cost £3000-£4,500 to install saving £17 per year.

The above examples were extracted from actual reports and will give an indication of cost and required improvements for specific property types.

Structural surveys

The basic structural survey is the homebuyers' survey and valuation, which is normally carried out by the building society or other lender and it will cost you between £200-350 and is not really an in-depth survey, merely allowing the lender to see whether they should lend or not and how much they should lend. Sometimes lenders keep what they refer to as a retention, which means that they will not forward the full value (less deposit) until certain defined works have been carried out.

If you want to go further than a homebuyers report, and the seller has not included a survey as part of the Home Information Pack (see below) then you will have to instruct a firm of surveyors who have several survey types, depending on how far you want to go and how much you want to spend.

A word of caution. Many people go rushing headlong into buying a flat or house. If you stop and think about this, it is complete folly and can prove very expensive later. A house or flat is a commodity like other commodities, except that it is usually a lot more expensive. A lot can be wrong with the commodity that you have purchased which is not immediately obvious. Only after you have completed the deal and paid over the odds for your purchase do you begin to regret what you have done.

The true market price of a property is not what the estate agent is asking, certainly not what the seller is asking. The true market price is the difference between what a property similar to the one in good condition is being sold at and your property minus cost of works to bring it up to that value.

Therefore, if you have any doubts whatsoever, and if you can afford it, get a detailed survey of the property you are proposing to buy and get the works that are required costed out. When negotiating, this survey is an essential tool in order to arrive at an accurate and fair price. Do not rest faith in others, particularly when you alone stand to lose.

One further word of caution. As stated, a lot of problems with property cannot be seen. A structural survey will highlight those. In some cases it may not be wise to proceed at all.

Mortgage arrangement fees

Depending upon the type of mortgage you are considering you may have to pay an arrangement fee. You should budget for anything up to 2% of the purchase price.

Other costs

You should factor in conveyancing costs which can be anything from £500-£1500 depending on the property that you purchase. The solicitor that you employ will give you an idea of the disbursements over and above the basic cost. These disbursements will cover searches of local authorities and utility companies plus other searches as necessary.

Now read the main points from chapter two.

Main points from chapter two

- Give careful thought to all the costs of buying property.

- Banks dealing with buy to let mortgages will normally lend between 65-75% of the purchase price of a property. The more that you lend the more it costs. Banks have now tightened their lending criteria following the credit crunch.

- If the house or flat costs over £125,000, stamp duty will be payable. There is no stamp duty payable for first time buyers on property up to £250,000 although this is due to revert to normal stamp duty after March 24th 2012.

- You should consider very carefully the need for a full structural survey when buying a property.

- Always bargain, never offer the asking price.

3

LOOKING FOR A PROPERTY- LOCATION AND TYPE

....

Obviously, where you choose to buy your property will be your own decision. However, it may be your first time and you may be at a loss as to where to buy, i.e. rural areas or urban areas, the type and cost of property or whether a house or flat. There are several considerations here. The main consideration for a buy-to-let property is the letting potential and security of your asset, i.e. will it appreciate or will it depreciate.

Area

Buying in a built up area has its advantages and disadvantages. There is usually more demand for property in a built up area. As far as letting is concerned, there are obvious advantages in that there are normally more close communities, because of the sheer density. Local services are closer to hand and there is a greater variety of housing for sale. Transport links are also usually quite good and there are normally plenty of shops.

Disadvantages are less space, less privacy, more local activity, noise and pollution, less street parking, more expensive insurance and different schooling environments to rural environments. The incidence of crime and vandalism and levels of overall stress are higher in built up, more urban areas. This is not the case with all built up areas. It is up to the buyer to carry out research before making a commitment.

If you are thinking of buying to let in a rural area, you might want to consider the following: There is more detached housing with land, more space and privacy. There is also cleaner air and insurance premiums can be lower.

Disadvantages can be isolation, loneliness, lower level of services generally, limited choice of local education, therefore the property will be harder to let.

Choosing your property

You should think carefully when considering purchasing a larger property. You may encounter higher costs prior to letting, and also costs that may deter the would be tenant, which may include:

- Larger more expensive carpeting.

- More furniture. If you are letting your property furnished then you will need to outlay more at the outset.

- Larger gardens to tend. Although this may have been one of the attractions, large gardens are time consuming, expensive and hard work.

- Bigger bills.

- More decorating.

- Higher overall maintenance costs.

Purchasing a flat

There are some important points to remember when purchasing a flat. These are common points that are overlooked. For example, if you are buying a flat in a block that is leasehold you will need permission to sublet. This may pose difficulties depending on the freeholder.

Service charge. If you purchase a flat in a block, the costs of maintenance of the flat will be your own. However, the costs of maintaining the common parts will be down to the landlord (usually) paid for by you through a service charge.

There has been an awful lot of trouble with service charges, trouble between landlord and leaseholder. It has to be said that many landlords see service charges as a way of making profit over and above other income, which is usually negligible after sale of a lease.

Many landlords will own the companies that carry out the work and retain the profit made by these companies. They will charge leaseholders excessively for works, which are often not needed. The 1996 Housing Act, amended by the 2002 Commonhold and Leasehold Reform Act, attempts to strengthen the hand of leaseholders against unscrupulous landlords by making it very difficult indeed for landlords to take legal action for forfeiture (repossession) of lease without first giving the leaseholder a chance to challenge the service charges. In addition, the Acts place an obligation on landlords to be more transparent by producing more detailed accounts and information.

Be very careful if you are considering buying a flat in a block. You should establish levels of service charges and look at accounts. Try to elicit information from other leaseholders.

It could be that there is a leaseholders organisation, formed to manage their own service charges. This will give you direct control over contracts such as gardening, cleaning, maintenance contracts and cyclical decoration contracts. Better value for money is obtained in this way. In this case, at least you know that the levels will be fair, as no one leaseholder stands to profit. All of the above should be considered as the profit that you make from letting your property can be greatly diminished by extra costs such as maintenance charges to a freeholder.

Leasehold Reform Act 1993

Under this Act, as amended by The Commonhold and Leasehold Reform Act 2002, all leaseholders have the right to extend the length of their lease by a term of 90 years. For example, if your lease has 80 years left to run you can extend it to 170 Years. There is a procedure in the above Act for valuation. Leaseholders can collectively also purchase the freehold of the block. There is a procedure for doing this in the Act although it is often time consuming and can be expensive. There are advantages however, particularly when leaseholders are not satisfied with management.

Viewing properties

Before you start house hunting, draw up a list of characteristics you will need from a property, such as the number of bedrooms, size of kitchen, garage and study and garden. Take the estate agents details with you when viewing. Also, take a tape measure with you.

Assess the location of the property. Look at all the aspects and the surroundings. Give some thought as to the impact this will have on the ability to rent.

Assess the building. Check the facing aspect of the property, i.e., north, south etc. Check the exterior carefully. Look for a damp proof course - normally about 15cm from the ground. Look for damp inside and out. Items like leaking rainwater pipes should be noted, as they can be a cause of damp. Look carefully at the windows. Are they rotten? Do they need replacing and so on. Look for any cracks. These should most certainly be investigated. A crack can be symptomatic of something worse or it can merely be surface. If you are not in a position to make this judgment then others should make it for you.

Heating is important. If the house or flat has central heating you will need to know when it was last tested. Gas central heating should be tested at least once a year.

All in all you need to remember that you cannot see everything in a house, particularly on the first visit. A great deal may be being concealed from you. In addition, your own knowledge of property may be slim. A second opinion is a must.

Buying a listed building

Buildings of architectural or historical interest are listed by the Secretary of State for National Heritage following consultation with English Heritage, to protect them against inappropriate alteration. In Wales, buildings are listed by the Secretary of State for Wales in consultation with CADW (Heritage Wales). In Scotland, they are listed by the Secretary of State for Scotland, in consultation with Historic Scotland. If you intend to carry out work to a listed building, you are likely to need listed building consent for any internal or external work, in addition to planning permission. The conservation officer in the local planning department can provide further information.

Buildings in conservation areas

Local authorities can designate areas of special architectural or historical significance. Conservation areas are protected to ensure that their character or interest is retained. Whole towns or villages may be conservation areas or simply one particular street.

Strict regulations are laid down for conservation areas. Protection includes all buildings and all types of trees that are larger than 7cm across at 1.5m above the ground. There may be limitations for putting up signs, outbuilding or items such as satellite dishes. Any developments in the area usually have to meet strict criteria, such as the use of traditional or local materials.

This also applies to property in national parks, designated areas of outstanding natural beauty and the Norfolk or Suffolk Broads.

Whether or not a property is listed or is deemed to be in a conservation area will show up when your conveyancer carries out the local authority search.

Buying a new house

There are a number of benefits to buying a new house. You have the advantages of being the first owner. There should not be a demand for too much maintenance or DIY jobs, as the building is new.

There will however be a defects period, which usually runs for 6 months for building and 12 months for electrical mechanical. During this period you should expect minor problems, such as cracking of walls, plumbing etc, which will be the responsibility of the builder.

Energy loss will be minimal. A new house today uses 50 per cent less energy than a house built 15 years ago; consider the savings over an older property.

An energy rating indicates how energy efficient a house is. The National House Building Council uses a rating scheme based on The National Energy Services Scheme, in which houses are given a rating between 0 and 10. A house rated 10 will be very energy efficient and have very low running costs for its size. In addition, an Energy Performance Certificate is mandatory, as described earlier. Security and safety are built in to new houses, smoke alarms are standard and security locks on doors and windows are usually included.

When the house market is slow, developers usually offer incentives to buyers, such as cash back, payment of deposit etc.

Building Guarantees

All new houses should be built to certain standards and qualify for one of the building industry guarantees. These building guarantees are normally essential for you to obtain a mortgage and they also make the property attractive to purchasers when you sell. A typical guarantee is the National House Building Council Guarantee (NHBCG).

Now read the main points from chapter three.

Main points from chapter three

- When looking for a house, consider essential points such as area and services and the impact these will have on letting.

- Think carefully about costs involved and also work if you are considering buying a larger property.

- When purchasing a flat, consider maintenance charges as these can eat into your profit.

- Before viewing, draw up a list of characteristics you will need from a house or flat.

- There are a number of advantages to buying a new house, such as new construction and minimal energy loss.

4

THE PROCESS OF BUYING A PROPERTY

....

Having considered the costs of the acquisition of a property, the next step is to find the property you want. For the investor, as well as all the considerations listed below, the return on investment will be a key priority.

Looking for a property is a long and sometimes dispiriting process. Trudging around estate agents, sorting through mountains of literature, dealing with estate agents details, scouring the papers and walking the streets. However, most of us find the property we want at the end of the day. It is then that we can put in our offer.

Making an offer

You should put your offer in to the estate agent or direct to the seller, depending on who you are buying from.

As discussed earlier, your offer should be based on sound judgment, on what the property is worth and how much rental income after costs that you can derive from it, not on your desire to secure the property at any cost. A survey will help you to arrive at a schedule of works and cost. If you cannot afford to employ a surveyor from a high street firm then you should try to enlist other help. In addition, you should take a long and careful look at the house yourself, not just a cursory glance. Look at everything and try to get an idea of the likely cost to you of rectifying defects. However, I cannot stress enough the importance of getting a detailed survey.

Eventually, you will be in a position to make an offer for the property. You should base this offer on sound judgment. You should make it clear that your offer is subject to contract and survey (if you require further examination or wish to carry out a survey after the offer).

Exchange of contracts

Once the buyer and seller are happy with all the details stated in the contract and your conveyancer can confirm that there are no outstanding legal queries, there will be an exchange of contracts. The sale is now legally binding for both parties. You should arrange the necessary insurances, buildings and contents from this moment on, as you are now responsible for the property.

Completing a sale

This is the final day of the sale and normally takes place around ten days after exchange. Exchange and completion can take place on the same day if necessary but this is unusual. On the day of completion, you are entitled to vacant possession and you will receive the keys.

Buying a property at an auction

Property can be purchased in an auction. A small amount of properties are sold in this way. Usually properties sold at auction are either unusual or difficult to put a price on or are repossessions. Auction lists can be obtained from larger estate agents or are advertised in papers. The Estates Gazette, published by the Royal Institute of Chartered Surveyors gives details of auctions in each publication. Normally, this magazine is available to subscribers only, although it can be ordered through a newsagent.

Preparing for auction

Because the auction is the final step of the sale, you should have any conveyancing carried out and your mortgage arranged. Auctions are a quick way of finding a property if you want to buy at undervalue and then renovate the property. It is likely that your choice of property may be limited and you will need to work on it. Many properties at auction are sub standard, this is why they are there in the first place.

- Ask for the package compiled by the auctioneer. It will include full details of the property, and the memorandum of agreement, which is equivalent to the contract.
- View the house.
- Organise a conveyancer and instruct him to carry out searches and arrange surveys.
- If you like the property, set yourself a price limit to bid to, and arrange a mortgage.

Buying before auction

If the sale details quote "unless previously sold" the seller may be prepared to accept offers before the auction, but he will still accept a fast sale and you will be signing an auction contract. You will need to arrange conveyancing and finance very quickly. If you are buying at the auction itself, you should remember that the fall of the hammer on your bid is equivalent to the exchange of contracts as for a private sale. You have made a legal arrangement and you will be expected to pay 10-15 percent deposit on the spot with the remainder of the payment within 28 days.

At the auction

If you are doubtful about your own ability then you can appoint a professional to act on your behalf although they will obviously charge for their services. The seller may be selling subject to a reserve price. If this is the case, it is normally stated in the particulars. The actual figure is not usually disclosed but if the auctioneer states something like "I am going to sell this property today" it is an indication that the reserve price has been reached.

Sale by tender

As an alternative to auction, sale by tender is like a blind auction; you don't know what the other potential buyers are offering. A form of tender is included in the sales details and sometimes sets out the contract details. Always check these details with your conveyancer, because often you cannot pull out after the offer is accepted.

Buyers put their offers in an envelope, sometimes with a 10 percent deposit. These must be received by the seller's agent at a specified date, at which time the seller will accept one of the offers. Sale by tender is sometimes used when there have been two or three offers at similar prices.

Now read the main points from chapter four.

Main points from chapter four

- Make an offer on what you think the property is worth and not the asking price.

- Look over the property you wish to buy very carefully indeed.

- If you are buying at an auction take great care.

The Property Investors Management Handbook

5

FINDING A TENANT

....

Having laid out your business plan, based on the considerations outlined in chapter one, and given much thought to the purchase of a property to let, it is now necessary to look at the possible sources of the tenant for your property. Remember, the tenant is the key to your future income and profit and also to your own personal peace or otherwise and therefore must be chosen extremely carefully. On the basis of your business plan you will know the type of person that you are prepared to accept because you will have identified what type of management scenario you wish. You will know their position, i.e., whether professional, student, working or on benefits or retired. In order to locate this person you will need to know the various sources available to you.

Letting Agents

There are obvious advantages in using an agent: they are likely to have tenants on their books: They are likely to be experienced and can vet tenants properly before signing a tenancy; they can provide you with a tenancy agreement and they can provide a service after the property is let. However, agents charge for this service and their fees can vary enormously. It is up to you as a would-be landlord to ensure you understand what it is they are charging and exactly what you are left with after the charges.

Some agencies will offer a guaranteed income for the duration of the contract that you have signed with them, even if a tenant leaves. However, you should be extremely careful as a number of cases recently against such agencies have revealed that there are unscrupulous operators around.

If you do appoint an agent to manage a property you should agree at the outset, in writing, exactly what constitutes management. Failure to understand the deal between you and the agent can cost you dearly. For example, in a lot of cases, an agent will charge you a fixed fee, sometimes 1 months rental, for finding a tenant, but will then exercise the right that they have given themselves in the initial contract to sign a new agreement and charge another months rent after the tenancy has expired. In this way they will charge you a months rent every six months for doing nothing at all.

Agents will typically look after the following:

1   Transfer the utility bills and the council tax into the name of the tenant. Sign agreements and take up references.
2   Paying for repairs, although an agent will only normally do this if rent is being paid directly to them and they can make appropriate deductions.
3   Chase rent arrears.
4   Serve notices of intent to seek possession if the landlord instructs them to do so. An agent cannot commence court proceedings except through a solicitor.
5   Visit the property at regular intervals and check that the tenants are not causing any damage.
6   Dealing with neighbour complaints.
7   Banking rental receipts if the landlord is abroad

8   Dealing with housing benefit departments if necessary. The extent to which agents actually do any or all of the above really depends on the caliber of the agent. It also depends on the type of agreement you have with the agent. Like your initial business plan, you should be very clear about what it is you want from the agent and how much they charge.

Beware! There are many so-called rental agencies, which have sprang up since the property recession and also the advent of "Buy to Let". These agents are not professional, do not know a thing about property management, are shady and should be avoided like the plague. Shop around and seek a reputable agent.

A typical management fee might be 10-15 percent of the rent, although there is lots of competition and lower prices can be obtained. As stated, there are many ways of charging and you should be clear about this. It is illegal for agencies to charge tenants for giving out a landlord's name and address. Most agencies will charge the landlord.

Advertisements

The classified advertisement section of local papers is a good place to seek potential tenants, particularly if you wish to avoid agency charges. Local papers are obviously cheaper than the nationals such as the Evening Standard in London or the broadsheets such as the Guardian. The type of newspaper you advertise in will largely reflect what type of customer you are looking for. An advert in the pages of the Times would indicate that you are looking for a well-heeled professional and this would be reflected in the type of property that you have to let.

There are many free ad papers and also you may want to go to student halls of residence or hospitals in order to attract a potential tenant.

When you do advertise, you should indicate clearly the type of property, in what area, what is required, i.e., male or female only, and the rent. You should try and avoid abbreviations as this causes confusion.

The public sector

One other source of income is the local authority or housing association. Quite often, your property will be taken off your hands under a five-year contract and you will receive a rental income paid direct for this period, with agreed increases. However, the local authority or housing association will demand a high standard before taking the property off your hands and quite often the rent achieved will be lower than a comparable market rent, in return for full management and secure income.

If you wish to try this avenue then you should contact your local authority or nearest large association.

Company lets

Where the tenant is a company rather than an individual, the tenancy agreement will be similar to an assured shorthold but will not be bound by the six-month rule (see chapter eight for details of assured shorthold tenancies). Company lets can be from any length of time, from a week to several years, or as long as you like.

The major difference between contracts and standard assured shorthold agreements is that the contract will be tailored to individual needs, and the agreement is bound by the provisions of contract law. Company tenancies are bound by the provisions of contract law and not by the Housing Acts. Note: if you are considering letting to a company you must use a letting agent or solicitor. Most companies will insist on it. The advantages of a landlord letting to a company are:

- A company or embassy has no security of tenure and therefore cannot be a sitting tenant.
- A company cannot seek to reduce the rent by statutory interventions.
- Rental payments are often made quarterly or six monthly in advance.
- The financial status of a company is usually more secure than that of an individual.
- Company tenants often require long-term lets to accommodate staff relocating on contracts of between one and five years.

The main disadvantages of company lets are:

- A company tenancy can only be to a bona fide company or embassy, not to a private individual.
- A tenancy to a partnership would not count as a company let and may have some security of tenure.
- If the tenant is a foreign government, the diplomatic status of the occupant must be ascertained, as the courts cannot enforce breaches of contract with somebody who possesses diplomatic immunity.
- A tenancy to a foreign company not registered in the UK may prove time consuming and costly if it becomes necessary to pursue claims for unpaid rent or damage through foreign courts.

Short-lets

Although company lets can be of any length, it is becoming increasingly popular for companies to rent flats from private landlords on short-lets. A short-let is any let of less than six months. But here, it is essential to check the rules with any borough concerned. Some boroughs will not allow lets for less than three months, as they do not want to encourage transient people in the neighborhood.

Generally speaking, short-lets are only applicable in large cities where there is a substantial shifting population. Business executives on temporary relocation, actors and others involved in television production or film work, contract workers and visiting academics are examples of people who might require a short-let.

From a landlord's point of view, short-lets are an excellent idea if you have to vacate your own home for seven or eight months, say, and do not want to leave it empty for that time. Short-let tenants provide useful extra income as well as keeping an eye on the place. Or if you are buying a new property and have not yet sold the old one, it can make good business sense to let it to a short-let tenant.

Short-let tenants are, usually, from a landlord's point of view, excellent blue-chip occupants. They are busy professionals, high earners, out all day and used to high standards. As the rent is paid by the company there is no worry for the landlord on this score either.

A major plus of short-lets is that they command between 20-50 percent more rent than the optimum market rent for that type of property. The one downside of short-lets is that no agency can guarantee permanent occupancy.

Student lets

Many mainstream letting agencies will not consider students and a lot of landlords similarly are not keen. There is the perception that students will not look after a home and tend to live a lifestyle guaranteed to increase the wear and tear on a property. However, if handled correctly, student lets can be profitable and a number of specialist companies have grown up which concentrate solely on students. Although students quite often want property for only eight or nine months, agencies that deal with students make them sign for a whole year. Rent is guaranteed by confirmation that the student is a genuine student with references from parents, who act as guarantors.

There can be a lot of money made from student lets. However, the tenancy will require more avid policing because of the nature of student lifestyle.

The DSS and housing benefit

Very few letting agencies or landlords will touch DSS or housing benefit tenants. However, as with student lets, there is another side of the coin.

Quite often it is essential for a tenant on HB to have a guarantor, usually a homeowner, before signing a tenancy. Then it is up to the machinations of the benefit system to ensure that the landlord receives rent. The rent is assessed by a benefit officer, with the rent usually estimated at market price. There are rent levels set for each are that the benefit officer will not go above. At the time of writing (2012) the benefit system is undergoing significant changes which will have an adverse impact on those on housing benefit and could also impact on those landlords who take tenants on HB.

A deposit is paid normally and rent is paid direct to the landlord. This will require the tenant's consent No other conditions should be accepted by a private landlord. Rent certainly should not be paid direct to the tenant.

Although tenants on HB have a bad name, due to stereotyping, there are many reasons why a person may be on benefit and if housing benefit tenancies are managed well, then this can be a useful source of tenant.

Holiday lets

Before the Housing Act 1988 became law, many landlords advertised their properties as holiday lets to bypass the then rules regarding security of tenure. Strictly speaking, a holiday let is a property let for no more than a month to any one tenant. If the same tenant renews for another month then the landlord is breaking the law. Nowadays, holiday lets must be just that; let for a genuine holiday.

If you have a flat or cottage that you wish to let for holiday purposes, whether or not you live in it yourself for part of the year, you are entering into a quite different agreement with the tenant.

Holiday lets are not covered by the Housing Act. The contract is finalised by exchange of letters with the tenant where they place a deposit and the owner confirms the booking. If the let is not for a genuine holiday you may have problems in evicting the tenant, as the whole point of a holiday let is that it is for no more than a fixed period of a month.

Generally speaking, certain services must be provided for the let to be deemed a holiday let. Cleaning services and changes of bed linen are essential. The amount paid by the holiday-maker will usually include utilities but would exclude use of the telephone, fax machine etc.

If you have a property that you think is suitable for holiday let or wish to invest in one, there are numerous companies who will put you on to their books. However, standards are high and there are a certain number of criteria to be met, such as safety checks, before they will consider taking you on.

If possible, you should talk to someone with some experience of this type of let before entering into an agreement with an agency. The usual problems may arise, such as ensuring occupancy all year round and the maintenance of your property, which will be higher due to a high turnover. In addition to the above, the tax situation is changing for those with holiday lets which will mean the loss of certain allowances and the tightening up of others.

Bedsits

Bedsitting rooms are usually difficult to let and can cause problems. It is best to leave this area of letting alone. There are numerous regulations to adhere to. Houses in Multiple Occupation regulations are quite strict.

The Housing Act 2004 has introduced new tougher regulations for HMOs. If a landlord is letting out property in a block with more than three unrelated dwellings then a licence will be needed from the local authority before lettings can take place. You should contact your local authority if you are in this position. There is also a problem of high turnover. Leave this kind of letting to others and concentrate on houses or flats.

Showing the property to the tenant

Once you have found a tenant, the next stage is to make arrangements for viewing the property. It is a good idea to make all appointments on the same day in order to avoid wasting time. If you decide on a likely tenant, it is wise to take up references yourself if you are not using an agency who will do this for you. This will normally be a previous landlord's reference and also a bank reference plus a personal reference.

Only when these have been received and you have established that the person(s) is/are safe should you go ahead. Make sure that no keys have been handed over until the cheque has been cleared and you are in receipt of a month's rent and a month's deposit.

Deposits

Tenancy Deposit Protection Scheme

The Tenancy Deposit Protection Scheme was introduced to protect all deposits paid to landlords after 6th April 2007. After this date, landlords and/or agents must use a government authorised scheme to protect deposits. The need for such a scheme has arisen because of the historical problem with deposits and the abuse of deposits by landlords.

The scheme works as follows:

Moving into a property

At the beginning of a new tenancy agreement, the tenant will pay a deposit to the landlord or agent as usual. Within 14 days the landlord is required to give the tenant details of how the deposit is going to be protected including:

- the contact details of the tenancy deposit scheme
- the contact details of landlord or agent

- how to apply for the release of the deposit
- what to do if there is a dispute about the deposit

There are three tenancy deposit schemes that a landlord can opt for:

Tenancy Deposit Solutions Ltd
www.mydeosits.co.uk
info@mydeposits.co.uk

The Tenancy Deposit Scheme
www.tds.gb.com
0845 226 7837

The Deposit Protection Service
www.depositprotection.com
0870 707 1 707

The schemes above fall into two categories, insurance based schemes and custodial schemes.

Custodial Scheme

- The tenant pays the deposit to the landlord
- The landlord pays the deposit into the scheme
- Within 14 days of receiving the deposit, the landlord must give the tenant prescribed information
- A the end of the tenancy, if the landlord and tenant have agreed how much of the deposit is to be returned, they will tell the scheme which returns the deposit, divided in the way agreed by the parties.

- If there is a dispute, the scheme will hold the disputed amount until the dispute resolution service or courts decide what is fair
- The interest accrued by deposits in the scheme will be used to pay for the running of the scheme and any surplus will be used to offer interest to the tenant, or landlord if the tenant isn't entitled to it.

Insurance based schemes
- The tenant pays the deposit to the landlord
- The landlord retains the deposit and pays a premium to the insurer (this is the key difference between the two schemes)
- Within 14 days of receiving a deposit the landlord must give the tenant prescribed information.
- At the end of the tenancy if the landlord and tenant agree how the deposit is to be divided or otherwise then the landlord will return the amount agreed
- If there is a dispute, the landlord must hand over the disputed amount to the scheme for safekeeping until the dispute is resolved
- If for any reason the landlord fails to comply, the insurance arrangements will ensure the return of the deposit to the tenant if they are entitled to it.

If a landlord or agent hasn't protected a deposit with one of the above then the tenant can apply to the local county court for an order for the landlord either to protect the deposit or repay it.

Rental guarantees

The landlord is always advised to obtain a guarantor if there is any potential uncertainty as to payment of rent. One example is where the tenant is on benefits. The guarantor will be expected to assume responsibility for the rent if the tenant ceases to pay at any time during the term of the tenancy. There is a sample guarantee form in the appendix to this book.

Be strictly business like. You are letting property for a profit and the tenants are the key to that profit. A mistake at the outset can cost you dearly for a long time to come. See chapter 13 and 15 for further information concerning the start of the tenancy.

In chapter six we will explore the legal framework governing residential lettings.

Now read the main points from chapter five.

Main points from chapter five

- The right choice of tenant is crucial as this is the key to the return on your investment.

- You should make sure that you have all the facts about a letting agents terms and conditions before you enter into an agreement.

- The classified advertisement section in the local paper is a good place to seek potential tenants, especially if you wish to manage the property yourself.

- The public sector offers a full management service but often offer a lower rent.

- There are other avenues to explore, such as company lets, short lets, holiday lets and so on. Make sure that you fully understand the various markets and what each entails before entering into an agreement.

- Make sure that, when you have found a tenant that you take up references and a deposit, and ensure that the tenant is fully aware of all relevant details.

6

WHAT SHOULD BE PROVIDED UNDER THE TENANCY?

....

Furniture

A landlords decision whether or not to furnish property will depend on the sort of tenant that he is aiming to find. The actual legal distinction between a furnished property and an unfurnished property has faded into insignificance.

If a landlord does let a property as furnished then the following would be the absolute minimum:

- Seating, such as a sofa and an armchair.

- Cabinet or sideboard.

- Kitchen tables and chairs.

- Cooker and refrigerator.

- Bedroom furniture.

Even unfurnished lets, however, are expected to come complete with a basic standard of furniture, particularly carpets and kitchen goods. If the landlord does supply electrical equipment then he or she will be responsible for carrying out annual checks along with annual checks on the boiler.

Services

Service charges, and the paying of these charges, will be the responsibility of the leaseholder of a flat and will be included in the rent charged by the leaseholder to the tenant of the flat. However, the leaseholder should have some idea of the law in this area as it will be a cost which needs to be considered.

Usually, a landlord (freeholder) will only provide services to a tenant if the property is a flat situated in a block or house split into flats or is a house on a private estate. The services will include cyclical painting and maintenance, usually on a three to four year basis (flats) and gardening and cleaning plus repairs to the communal areas, plus communal electricity bills and water rates. These services should be outlined in the agreement and administered within a strict framework of law. The 1985 Landlord and Tenant Act Section 18-30 as amended by the 1987 LTA and the 1996 Housing Act as amended by the 2002 Commonhold and Leasehold Reform Act are the main areas of law.

The landlord has rigid duties imposed within the Acts, such as the need to gain estimates before commencing works and also to consult with residents where the cost exceeds £250 per flat. The landlord must give the tenant 28 days notice of works to be carried out and a further 28 days to consider estimates, inviting feedback.

Tenants (leaseholders) have the right to see audited accounts and invoices relating to work. Service charges, as an extra payment over and above the rent are always contentious and it is an area that landlords need to be aware of if they are to manage professionally.

Repairs

See chapter on repairs and improvements.

Insurance

Strictly speaking, there is no legal duty on either landlord or tenant to insure the property. However, it is highly advisable for the landlord to provide buildings insurance as he/she stands to lose a lot more in the event of fire or other disaster than the tenant. In addition, mortgagors will always want insurance in place to protect their own investment.

A landlord letting property for a first time would be well advised to consult his/her insurance company before letting as there are different criteria to observe when a property is let and not to inform the company could invalidate the policy.

At the end of the tenancy

The tenancy agreement will normally spell out the obligations of the tenant at the end of the term. Essentially, the tenant will have an obligation to:

- Have kept the interior clean and tidy and in a good state of repair and decoration.

- Have not caused any damage.

- Have replaced anything that they have broken.

- Replace or pay for the repair of anything that they have damaged.
- Pay for the laundering of the linen.

57

- Pay for any other laundering.

- Put anything that they have moved or removed back to how it was.

Sometimes a tenancy agreement will include for the tenants paying for anything that is soiled at their own expense, although sensible wear and tear is allowed for. The landlord will normally be able to recover any loss from the deposit that the tenant has given on entering the premises (see previous chapter for details of the Deposit Protection Schemes). However, sometimes, the tenants will withhold rent for the last month in order to recoup their deposit. The introduction of the Deposit Protection Schemes have made this more difficult in practice. It is up to the landlord to negotiate reimbursement for any damage caused, but this should be within reason. There is a remedy, which can be pursued in the small claims court if the tenants refuse to pay but this is rarely successful.

Now read the main points from chapter six.

Main points from chapter Six

- A landlord's decision to furnish a property will depend on the sort of tenant he is aiming to find.

- Even unfurnished lets are expected to come complete with a basic standard of furniture.

- Usually, the landlord (freeholder) will only supply services to a tenant if the flat is in a block or a house on a private estate.

- If services are provided tenants (leaseholders) have a right to audited accounts annually. The extra burden of service charges should be taken into account when letting the property.

7

THE LAW IN A NUTSHELL

....

Explaining the law

Having traveled this far in finding a property and a tenant, and signed up the tenant, it is now time to understand a little more about the law.

As a landlord or potential landlord it is very important to understand the rights and obligations of both yourself and your tenant, exactly what can and what cannot be done once the tenancy agreement has been signed and the tenant has moved into the property.

Some landlords think they can do exactly as they please, because the property belongs to them. Tenants often do not know any differently and therefore the landlord can, and often does, get away with breaking the law. However, if you are about to embark upon a career as a landlord, letting property for profit, then it is important that you have a grasp of the key principles of the law. In order to fully understand the law we should begin by looking at the main types of relationship between people and their homes.

The freehold and the lease

In law, there are two main types of ownership and occupation of property. These are: freehold and leasehold. These arrangements are very old indeed.

Freehold

If a person owns their property outright (usually with a mortgage) then they will be a freeholder.

The only claims to ownership over and above their own might be those of the building society or the bank, which lent them the money to buy the place. They will re-possess the property if the mortgage payments are not kept up with.

In certain situations though, the local authority (council) for an area can affect a person's right to do what they please with their home even if they are a freeholder. This will occur when planning powers are exercised, for example, in order to prevent the carrying out of alterations without consent.

The local authority for your area has many powers and we will be referring to these regularly in each chapter of this guide.

Leasehold

If a person lives in a property owned by someone else and has a written agreement allowing them to occupy the flat or house for a period of time i.e., giving them permission to live in that property, then they will, in the main, have a lease and either be a leaseholder or a tenant of a landlord.

The main principle of a lease is that a person has been given permission by someone else to live in his or her property for a period of time. The person giving permission could be either the freeholder or another leaseholder.

The tenancy agreement is one type of lease. If you have issued a tenancy agreement then you will have given permission to a person to live in your property for a period of time.

The position of the tenant

The tenant will usually have an agreement for a shorter period of time than the typical leaseholder. Whereas the leaseholder will, for example, have an agreement for ninety-nine years, the tenant will have an agreement, which either runs from week to week or month to month (periodic tenancy) or is for a fixed term, for example, six months. These arrangements are the most common types of agreement between the private landlord and tenant, with the six month assured shorthold being the usual tenancy offered..

The agreement itself will state whether it is a fixed term or periodic tenancy. If an agreement has not been issued it will be assumed to be a periodic tenancy.

Both periodic and fixed term tenants will usually pay a sum of rent regularly to a landlord in return for permission to live in the property. (More about rent and service charges later).

The tenancy agreement

The tenancy agreement is the usual arrangement under which one person will live in a property owned by another. Before a tenant moves into a property he/she will have to sign a tenancy agreement drawn up by a landlord or landlord's agent. A tenancy agreement is a contract between landlord and tenant.

The contract

Typically, any tenancy agreement will show the name and address of the landlord and will state the names of the tenant(s). The type of tenancy agreement that is signed should be clearly indicated. This could be, for example, a Rent Act protected tenancy, an assured tenancy or an assured shorthold tenancy. In the main, the agreement will be an assured shorthold. The date the tenancy began and the duration (fixed term or periodic) plus the amount of rent payable should be clearly shown along with who is responsible for any other charges, such as water rates, council tax etc, and a description of the property you are renting out.

In addition to the rent that must be paid there should be a clear indication of when a rent increase can be expected. This information is sometimes shown in other conditions of tenancy, which should be given to the tenant when they move into their home. The conditions of tenancy will set out landlords and tenants rights and obligations.

If services are provided, i.e., if a service charge is payable, this should be indicated in the agreement. The tenancy agreement should indicate clearly the address to which notices on the landlord can be served by the tenant, for example, because of repair problems or notice of leaving the property. The landlord has a legal requirement to indicate this.

The tenancy agreement will either be a basic document with the above information or will be more comprehensive. Either way, there will be a section beginning "the tenant agrees." Here the tenant will agree to move into the property, pay rent, use the property as an only home, not cause a nuisance to others, take responsibility for certain internal repairs, not sublet the property, i.e., create another tenancy, and various other things depending on the property. There should also be another section "the landlord agrees". Here, the landlord is contracting with the tenant to allow quiet enjoyment of the property. The landlord's repairing responsibilities are also usually outlined.

Finally, there should be a section entitled "ending the tenancy" which will outline the ways in which landlord and tenant can end the agreement. It is in this section that the landlord should make reference to the "grounds for possession". Grounds for possession are circumstances where the landlord will apply to court for possession of his/her property. Some of these grounds relate to what is in the tenancy, i.e., the responsibility to pay rent and to not cause a nuisance.

Other grounds do not relate to the contents of the tenancy directly, but more to the law governing that particular tenancy. The grounds for possession are very important, as they are used in any court case brought against the tenant. Unfortunately, they are not always indicated in the tenancy agreement. As they are so important they are summarized later on in this chapter.

It must be said at this point that many residential tenancies are very light on landlord's responsibilities. Repairing responsibilities, and responsibilities relating to rental payment, are landlords obligations under law. This book deals with these, and other areas. However, many landlords will seek to use only the most basic document in order to conceal legal obligations.

The public sector tenancy (local authority or housing association), for example, is usually very clear and very comprehensive about the rights and obligations of landlord and tenant. Unfortunately, the private landlord often does not employ the same energy when it comes to educating and informing the tenant. This is one of the main reasons for this book. It is essential that those who intend to let property for profit are able to manage professionally and set high standards as a private landlord. This is because the sector has been beset by rogues in the past. Appendix 1 shows what a typical residential tenancy agreement should look like.

The responsibility of the landlord to provide a tenant with a rent book

If the tenant is a weekly periodic tenant the landlord must provide him/her with a rent book and commits a criminal offence if he/she does not do so. This is outlined in the Landlord and Tenant Act 1985 sections 4-7. Under this Act any tenant can ask in writing the name and address of the landlord. The landlord must reply within twenty-one days of asking.

As most tenancies nowadays are fixed term assured shortholds then it is not strictly necessary to provide a tenant with a rent book. However, for the purposes of business efficiency, and your own records, it is always useful to issue a rent book to tenants and sign it each time rent is collected or a standing order is paid.

Overcrowding and the rules governing too many people living in the property

It is important to understand, when signing a tenancy agreement, that it is not permitted to allow the premises to become overcrowded, i.e., to allow more people than was originally intended, (which is outlined in the agreement) to live in the property. If a tenant does then the landlord can take action to evict.

Different types of tenancy agreement
The protected tenancy agreement
There are still a very few agreements that were signed prior to 1989 and they will be protected. However, as these are diminishing in number it is not intended to concentrate on these any further.

The assured tenancy agreement - what it means

If the tenant entered into an agreement with a landlord after 15th January 1989 then they will, in most cases, be an assured tenant. We will discuss assured tenancies in more depth in chapter eight. In brief, there are various types of assured tenancy. The assured shorthold is usually a fixed term version of the assured tenancy and enables the landlord to recover their property after six months and to vary the rent after this time.

At this point it is important to understand that the main difference between the two types of tenancy, protected and assured, is that the tenant has less rights as a tenant under the assured tenancy. For example, they will not be entitled, as is a protected tenant, to a fair rent set by a rent officer.

Other types of agreement

In addition to the above tenancy agreements, there are other types of agreement sometimes used in privately rented property. One of these is the company let, as we discussed in chapter five, and another is the license agreement. The person signing such an agreement is called a licensee. Licenses will only apply in special circumstances where the licensee cannot be given sole occupation of his home and therefore can only stay for a short period with minimum rights. It is not the intention to pursue licensees further in this book.

The squatter (trespasser)

In addition to the tenant and licensee, there is one other type of occupation of property, which needs mentioning. This is squatting. It is useful for the would-be landlord to have a basic understanding of this area of occupation.

The squatter is usually someone who has gained entry to a vacant property, either a house or a flat, without permission.

Although the squatter, a trespasser, has the protection of the law and cannot be evicted without a court order, if he or she is to be given the protection of the law, the squatted property must have been empty in the first place.

On gaining entry to a property, the squatter will normally put up a notice claiming squatter's rights, which means that they are identifying themselves as a person or group having legal protection until a court order is obtained to evict them. Even if no notice is visible, the squatter has protection and it is an offence to attempt to remove them forcibly.

The squatter has protection from eviction under the Protection from Eviction Act 1977 and is also protected from violence or harassment by the Criminal Law Act of 1977.

The trespasser who has entered an occupied property without permission has fewer rights. Usually, the police will either arrest or escort a trespasser off the premises. There is no protection from eviction. However, there is protection from violence and intimidation under the Criminal Law Act of 1977.

Currently, there is a bill going through parliament which will make the action of squatting a criminal offence. At the time of writing this is still going through the process.

Now read the main points from chapter seven

Main points from chapter seven

- **Private Tenant.** A tenant of a landlord who is not a public landlord, public landlord being for example a local authority or housing association. The most common private tenancy relationship is between two individuals or between an individual and a company.

- **Leasehold and freehold.** These are the two main types of ownership of land and occupation of property. A freeholder will own the property outright (usually with a mortgage). A leaseholder has the right to live there for a period of time.

- **Tenancy agreement.** The tenancy agreement is one form of lease. It is a contract between the landlord and tenant for the occupation of property. The tenancy agreement is either for a specific length (e.g., six months) of time or from week to week or month to month. The agreement will govern the length of notice given by the landlord or tenant when requiring the property back, or in the case of the tenant, leaving the property.

- **Rent book.** If a tenancy is a weekly periodic tenancy, then a landlord must provide a tenant with a rent book.

- **Overcrowding.** A tenant must not allow his/her home to become overcrowded. A landlord can take a tenant to court and can evict in this case.

- **The assured tenant.** This is the usual type of tenancy agreement entered into after 15th January 1989, which is

69

regulated by the 1988 Housing Act (as amended). In chapter eight we discuss this type of agreement.

- **The licence and the licensee.** This is one type of agreement between landlord and tenant, which gives the occupier fewer rights than a protected tenant.

- **The squatter (trespasser).** The squatter is someone who has entered a vacant property without permission and set up home there. The squatter can be evicted only with a court order. However, someone who has entered an occupied property, has no protection at all and can be removed immediately by the police.

8

ASSURED TENANTS

....

The assured tenant

As we discussed in chapter seven, all tenancies, with the exceptions detailed, entered into after 15th January 1989, are known as assured tenancies. An **assured shorthold tenancy**, which is the most common form of tenancy used by the landlord nowadays, is one type of assured tenancy, and is for a fixed term of six months minimum and can be brought to an end with two months notice by serving a section 21 (of the Housing Act 1988) notice.

Assured tenancies are governed by the 1988 Housing Act, as amended by the 1996 Housing Act. It is to these Acts, or outlines of the Acts that the landlord must refer when intending to sign a tenancy and let a residential property.

For a tenancy to be assured, three conditions must be fulfilled:

1. The premises must be a dwelling house. This basically means any premises, which can be lived in. Business premises will normally fall outside this interpretation.
2. There must exist a particular relationship between landlord and tenant. In other words there must exist a tenancy agreement. For example, a licence to occupy, as in the case of students, or accommodation occupied as a result of work, cannot be seen as a tenancy. Following on from this, the accommodation must be let as

a single unit. The tenant, who must be an individual, must normally be able to sleep, cook and eat in the accommodation. Sharing of bathroom facilities will not prevent a tenancy being an assured tenancy but shared cooking or other facilities, such as a living room, will.

3. The third requirement for an assured tenancy is that the tenant must occupy the dwelling as his or her only or principal home. In situations involving joint tenants at least one of them must occupy.

Tenancies that are not assured

A tenancy agreement will not be assured if one of the following conditions applies:

- The tenancy or the contract was entered into before 15th January 1989.

- If no rent is payable or if only a low rent amounting to less than two thirds of the present ratable value of the property is payable.

- If the premises are let for business purposes or for mixed residential and business purposes.

- If part of the dwelling house is licensed for the sale of liquor for consumption on the premises. This does not include the publican who lets out a flat.

- If the dwelling house is let with more than two acres of agricultural land.

- If the dwelling house is part of an agricultural holding and is occupied in relation to carrying out work on the holding.

- If the premises are let by a specified institution to students, i.e., halls of residence.

- If the premises are let for the purpose of a holiday.

- Where there is a resident landlord, e.g., in the case where the landlord has let one of his rooms but continues to live in the house.

- If the landlord is the Crown (the monarchy) or a government department. Certain lettings by the Crown are capable of being assured, such as some lettings by the Crown Estate Commissioners.

- If the landlord is a local authority, a fully mutual housing association (this is where you have to be a shareholder to be a tenant) of a newly created Housing Action Trust or any similar body listed in the 1988 Housing Act.

- If the letting is transitional such as a tenancy continuing in its original form until phased out, such as a protected tenancy under the 1977 Rent Act.

- Secure tenancy granted before 15th January 1989, e.g., from a local authority or housing association. These tenancies are governed by the 1985 Housing Act).

The Assured Shorthold tenancy

The assured shorthold tenancy as we have seen, is the most common form of tenancy used in the private sector. The main principle of the assured shorthold tenancy is that it is issued for a period of six months minimum and can be brought to an end by the landlord serving two months notice on the tenant. At the end of the six-month period the tenant, if given two months prior notice, by the landlord serving a section 21 notice (see appendix) must leave.

The section 21 notice, so called because it arises out of Section 21 of the 1988 Housing Act, is the pro-forma that all landlords must use when ending a tenancy.

Any property let on an assured tenancy can be let on an assured shorthold, providing the following conditions are met:

- The tenancy must be for a fixed term of not less than six months.

- The agreement cannot contain powers, which enable the landlord to end the tenancy before six months. This does not include the right of the landlord to enforce the grounds for possession, which will be approximately the same as those for the assured tenancy (see below).

- A notice requiring possession at the end of the term is usually served two months before that date.

- A notice must be served before any rent increase giving one month's clear notice and providing details of the rent increase.

Getting possession of your property before the end of the tenancy

If the landlord wishes to get possession of his/her property, in this case before the expiry of the contractual term, the landlord has to gain a court order. A notice of seeking possession must be served, giving fourteen days notice and following similar grounds of possession as an assured tenancy (see below).

The landlord cannot simply tell a tenant to leave before the end of the agreed term.

A copy of a notice of seeking possession for an assured (shorthold) tenancy is shown in the Appendix.

Tenancy running on after fixed term

An assured shorthold tenancy will become periodic (will run from week to week) when the initial term of six months has elapsed and the landlord has not brought the tenancy to an end.

If the tenancy runs on after the end of the fixed term then the landlord can regain possession by giving the required two months notice, as mentioned above.

At the end of the term for which the assured shorthold tenancy has been granted, the landlord has an automatic right to possession.

Evicting assured shorthold tenants

As discussed, it is possible to gain possession of a property before the end of the fixed term if the tenancy has been seriously breached. Assured shorthold tenants, can be evicted only on certain grounds some discretionary, some mandatory (see below).

In order for the landlord of an assured shorthold tenant to regain

The Property Investors Management Handbook

possession of the property, using grounds for possession such as non-payment of rent, a notice of seeking possession (of property) must be served, giving fourteen days notice of expiry and stating the ground for possession.

Following the fourteen days a court order must be obtained. Although gaining a court order is not complicated, a solicitor will usually be used. Court costs can be awarded against the tenant.

Security of tenure: The ways in which a tenant can lose their home as an assured (shorthold) tenant

There are a number of circumstances called grounds (mandatory and discretionary) whereby a landlord can start a court action to evict a tenant.

The following are the mandatory grounds (where the judge must give the landlord possession) and discretionary grounds (where the judge does not have to give the landlord possession) on which a court can order possession if the home is subject to an assured tenancy.

The mandatory grounds for possession

There are eight mandatory grounds for possession, which, if proved, leave the court with no choice but to make an order for possession. It is very important that you understand these.

- *Ground One* is used where the landlord has served a notice, no later than at the beginning of the tenancy, warning the tenant that this ground may be used against him/her.
  This ground is used where the landlord wishes to recover the property as his or her principal (first and only) home or the spouse's

(wife's or husbands) principal home. The ground is not available to a person who bought the premises for gain (profit) whilst they were occupied.

- *Ground Two* is available where the property is subject to a mortgage and if the landlord does not pay the mortgage, could lose the home.

- *Grounds Three and Four* relate to holiday lettings.

- *Ground Five* is a special one, applicable to ministers of religion.

- *Ground Six* relates to the demolition or reconstruction of the property.

- *Ground Seven* applies if a tenant dies and in his will leaves the tenancy to someone else: but the landlord must start proceedings against the new tenant within a year of the death if he wants to evict the new tenant.

- *Ground Eight* concerns rent arrears. This ground applies if, both at the date of the serving of the notice seeking possession and at the date of the hearing of the action, the rent is at least 8 weeks in arrears or two months in arrears. This is the main ground used by landlords when rent is not being paid.

One of the advantages of a court order is that you will have details of the tenant's employers and can get an attachment of earnings against the tenant.

The discretionary grounds for possession of a property

As we have seen, the discretionary grounds for possession are those in relation to which the court has some powers over whether or not the landlord can evict. In other words, the final decision is left to the judge. Often the judge will prefer to grant a suspended order first, unless the circumstances are dramatic.

- *Ground Nine* applies when suitable alternative accommodation is available or will be when the possession order takes effect. As we have seen, if the landlord wishes to obtain possession of his or her property in order to use it for other purposes then suitable alternative accommodation has to be provided.

- *Ground Ten* deals with rent arrears as does ground eleven. These grounds are distinct from the mandatory grounds, as there does not have to be a fixed arrear in terms of time scale, e.g., 8 weeks. The judge, therefore, has some choice as to whether or not to evict. In practice, this ground will not be relevant to managers of assured shorthold tenancies.

- *Ground Twelve* concerns any broken obligation of the tenancy. As we have seen with the protected tenancy, there are a number of conditions of the tenancy agreement, such as the requirement not to racially or sexually harass a neighbour. Ground Twelve will be used if these conditions are broken.

- *Ground Thirteen* deals with the deterioration of the dwelling as a result of a tenant's neglect. This is connected with the structure of the property and is the same as for a protected tenancy. It puts the responsibility on the tenant to look after the premises.

- *Ground Fourteen* concerns nuisance, annoyance and illegal or immoral use. This is where a tenant or anyone connected with the tenant has caused a nuisance to neighbours.

- *Ground Fourteen A* this ground deals with domestic violence.

- *Ground Fifteen* concerns the condition of the furniture and tenants neglect. As Ground thirteen puts some responsibility on the tenant to look after the structure of the building so Ground Fifteen makes the tenant responsible for the furniture and fittings.

The description of the grounds above is intended as a guide only. For a fuller description please refer to the 1988 Housing Act, section 7, Schedule two,) as amended by the 1996 Housing Act) which is available at reference libraries.

As we have discussed, it is usual for the landlord of an assured shorthold tenancy to serve a notice requiring possession on the tenant giving two months notice. It is unusual for a landlord to take an assured shorthold tenant to court on one of the grounds for possession. However, these circumstances do arise, where a tenant has breached the tenancy very early on and the landlord cannot wait for the fixed term to expire.

Fast track possession

In November 1993, following changes to the County Court Rules, a facility was introduced which enables landlords of tenants with assured shorthold tenancies to apply for possession of their property without the usual time delay involved in waiting for a court date and attendance at court. This is known as "fast track possession" It cannot be used for rent arrears or other grounds. It is used to gain possession of a property when the fixed term of six months or more has come to an end, a valid section 21 notice has been served and the tenant will not move.

Raising rent

If the landlord wishes to raise rent, at least one month's minimum notice must be given. The rent cannot be raised more than once for the **same** tenant in one year. Tenants have the right to challenge a rent increase if they think it is unfair by referring the rent to a Rent Assessment Committee. The committee will prevent the landlord from raising the rent above the ordinary market rent for that type of property.

Now read the main points from chapter eight.

Main Points from Chapter Eight

- **Assured tenancies**. All tenancies signed after 15th January 1989, with a few exceptions, are assured tenancies. The assured shorthold tenancy is one type of assured tenancy and is the one most frequently used by private landlords.

- **Protection**. Assured tenancies are not protected by the 1977 Rent Act and do not have a right to a fair rent.

- **Security**. Assured tenants can only be evicted on certain grounds for possession, after being given a minimum of fourteen days notice and taken to court.

- **Rents**. Assured rents cannot be raised more than once in a one-year period for the same tenant. They can, however, be raised when a fixed term assured shorthold has ended. This may be after six months.

- **Fixed term**. An assured shorthold tenancy is granted for a minimum period of six months. Two months notice has to be given before ending the tenancy. The notice can be served when granting the tenancy bringing it to an end on the last day of the six months. After the six months has elapsed, two months notice can be given anytime. The tenancy can be allowed to run on, it becomes an assured shorthold periodic tenancy, as opposed to fixed term.

9

JOINT TENANCIES

....

Joint tenancies: the position of two or more people who have a tenancy agreement for one property

Although it is the normal state of affairs for a tenancy agreement to be granted to one person, this is not always the case.

A tenancy can also be granted to two or more people and is then known as a joint tenancy. The position of joint tenants is exactly the same as that of single tenants. In other words, there is still one tenancy even though it is shared.

Each tenant is responsible for paying the rent and observing the terms and conditions of the tenancy agreement. No one joint tenant can prevent another joint tenant's access to the premises.

If one of the joint tenants dies then his or her interest will automatically pass to the remaining joint tenants. A joint tenant cannot dispose of his or her interest in a will.

If one joint tenant, however, serves a notice to quit (notice to leave the property) on another joint tenant(s) then the tenancy will come to an end and the landlord can apply to court for a possession order, if the remaining tenant does not leave.

The position of a wife or husband in relation to joint tenancies is rather more complex because the married person has more rights when it comes to the home than the single person.

Remember, the position of a tenant who has signed a joint tenancy agreement is exactly the same as that of the single tenant. If one person leaves, the other(s) have the responsibilities of the tenancy. If one person leaves without paying his share of the rent then the other tenants will have to pay instead.

Now read the Main Points from Chapter Nine

- **Joint tenants.** A tenancy granted to two or more people is a joint tenancy. The position of joint tenants is exactly the same as that of a single tenant.

- **Ending the tenancy.** In order to end the tenancy, one of the joint tenants must serve a notice to quit on the other tenant(s).

10

RENT

The payment of rent and other financial matters

If a tenancy is protected under the Rent Act 1977, as described earlier there is the right to apply to the Rent Officer for the setting of a fair rent for the property.

The assured tenant

The assured (shorthold) tenant has far fewer rights in relation to rent control than the protected tenant.

The Housing Act 1988 allows a landlord to charge whatever he likes. There is no right to a fair or reasonable rent with an assured tenancy, which at this moment in time is very high, particularly in London. The rent can sometimes be negotiated at the outset of the tenancy. This rent has to be paid as long as the contractual term of the tenancy lasts. Once the contractual term has expired, the landlord is entitled to continue to charge the same rent.

On expiry of an assured shorthold the landlord is free to grant a new tenancy and set the rent to a level that is compatible with the market.

Rent control for assured shorthold tenants

We have seen that the assured shorthold tenancy is for a period of six months minimum. Like the assured tenant, the assured shorthold tenant has no right to request that a fair rent should be set. The rent is a market rent. As with an assured tenancy, the assured shorthold tenant has the right to appeal to a Rent Assessment Committee in the case of what he/she considers an unreasonable rent. This may be done during the contractual term of the tenancy. The Committee will consider whether the rent is significantly higher than is usual for a similar property.

If the Committee assesses a different rent from that set by the landlord, they may set a date when the increase will take effect. The rent cannot be backdated to before the date of the application. Once a decision has been reached by the Committee, the landlord cannot increase the rent for at least twelve months, or on termination of the tenancy.

Council tax and the tenant

Council tax is based on properties, or dwellings, and not individual people.

This means that there is one bill for each individual dwelling, rather than separate bills for each person. The number and type of people who live in the dwelling may affect the size of the final bill. A discount of 25 percent is given for people who live alone. Each property is placed in a valuation band with different properties paying more or less depending on their individual value. Tenants who feel that their home has been placed in the wrong valuation band can appeal to their local authority council tax department.

Who has to pay the council tax?

In most cases the tenant occupying the dwelling will have to pay the council tax. That person is known as the 'liable person'. Nobody under the age of 18 can be a liable person.

Couples living together will both be liable even if there is only one name appearing on the bill. However, a landlord will be responsible for paying the council tax where:

- there are several households living in one dwelling where households pay rent separately or;
- where people are under the age of 18;
- the people who live in the property are all asylum seekers who are not entitled to claim benefits including council tax benefits;
- the people who are staying in the property are there temporarily and have their main homes elsewhere; or
- the property is a care home, hospital, hostel or women's refuge.

Although the landlord has the responsibility for paying the council tax, he or she will normally try to pass on the increased cost through rents. However, there is a set procedure for a landlord to follow if he/she wishes to increase rent.

The rules covering council tax liability can be obtained from a Citizens Advice Bureau or from your local authority council tax department.

Service charges
What is a service charge?

A service charge covers a provision of services other than those covered by the rent. In practice, a leaseholder sub-letting his flat will also have to take into account service charges. A rental payment will normally cover maintenance charges, loan charges if any, and also profit. Other services, such as cleaning and gardening, will be covered by a separate charge, known as a service charge. A registered rent reflects the cost of any services provided by the landlord. An assured rent set by a landlord will normally include services which must be outlined in the agreement.

The fact that the charges are variable must be written into a tenancy agreement and the landlord has a legal duty to provide the tenant with annual budgets and accounts and has to consult when he or she wishes to spend over a certain amount of money, currently £250 per dwelling for major works such as decorating or £100 if the renewing a contract such as gardening, cleaning or lift maintenance, per scheme (estate or block of flats), whichever is the greater.

The form of consultation, which must take place, is that of writing to all those affected and informing them of:

- -The landlord's intention to carry out work (30 days notice).
- -Why these works are seen to be necessary.
- -The estimated cost of the works (further 30 days notice).
  -At least two estimates or the inviting of them to see two estimates.

The landlord can incur reasonable expense, without consultation, if the work is deemed to be necessary, i.e. emergency works.

If a service charge is variable then a landlord has certain legal obligations, which are clearly laid out in the 1985 and 1987 Landlord and Tenant Acts as amended by the 1996 Housing Act and the 2002 Commonhold and Leasehold Reform Act.

If you intend to let property for profit then it is of the utmost importance that you understand the law governing service charges.

Payment of housing benefit directly to the landlord

Housing benefit is a payment made to the tenant rather than the landlord. The amount of benefit that a tenant is paid will very much depend on that persons circumstances. The rules regarding payment of housing benefit have tightened considerably over the years and if you know that a tenant is going to be claiming housing benefit then you should be sure that they will be entitled. Local authorities have local rents that they will pay and they will not pay, for example, for a single person to occupy accommodation surplus to their needs or for anyone to claim what they see as excessive rent.

It is possible to arrange for the local authority to pay housing benefit direct to the landlord, especially where there are more than eight weeks in arrears. If there is an arrears problem and the landlord believes that the tenant is entitled to, or may be receiving housing benefit then the local authority should be contacted.

Housing benefit and possession for arrears of rent

Very often, problems in obtaining benefit will cause tenants to accrue rent arrears. If a landlord has let a property knowing that the tenant is claiming housing benefit it is better to wait for the tenant to sort it out. The court is unlikely to give possession if arrears are accruing because of benefit. Once there are eight weeks of arrears (see grounds for possession) then the court has no choice but to give possession anyway and quite often it is better to wait rather than jumping the gun and losing rental income altogether.

If on the other hand the tenant has stated that they are going to pay rent personally rather than benefit then the court will look more favorably on- giving possession to the landlord if arrears have arisen as a result of an immediate claim for benefit.

Now read the main points from chapter ten.

Main points from chapter ten

- **Fair rent.** If a tenancy is protected under the Rent Act 1977 there will be entitlement to a fair rent set by a Rent Officer.
- **Increase of fair rent.** Once the Rent Officer has set a fair rent the landlord cannot increase it unless he appeals.
- **Putting the rent up.** Even if the fair rent is higher than the existing rent, the landlord cannot charge more until the expiry of the two-year period.
- **Assured tenancies.** If a tenancy is assured there will not be the protection of the 1977 Rent Act and no entitlement to a fair rent. The rent charged would be a market rent.
- **Council tax.** If the tenant does not receive an individual bill for council tax then the landlord will be responsible for payment. This is usually the case in a multi-occupied home or block. The landlord cannot increase the rent without either notifying the Rent Officer or giving the required notice if an assured tenant.
- **Service charge.** A service charge is a charge for services such as cleaning or gardening. A landlord must show the cost of services clearly unless the total charge is less than 5 percent of rent. The service charge can be variable, e.g., varied once a year, or fixed, where it cannot be increased until the end of the two-year period.

11

THE RIGHT TO QUIET ENJOYMENT OF A HOME

....

Earlier, we saw that when a tenancy agreement is signed, the landlord is contracting to give quiet enjoyment of the tenants home. This means that they have the right to live peacefully in the home without harassment.

The landlord is obliged not to do anything that will disturb the right to the quiet enjoyment of the home. The most serious breach of this right would be for the landlord to wrongfully evict a tenant.

Eviction: what can be done against unlawful harassment and eviction
It is a criminal offence for a landlord to unlawfully evict a residential occupier (whether or not a tenant!). The occupier has protection under the Protection from Eviction Act 1977 section 1(2).

If the tenant or occupier is unlawfully evicted his/her first course should be to seek an injunction compelling the landlord to readmit him/her to the premises.

It is an unfortunate fact but many landlords will attempt to evict tenants forcefully. In doing so they break the law.

However, the landlord may, on termination of the tenancy recover possession without a court order if the agreement was entered into after 15th January 1989 and it falls into one of the following six situations:

- The occupier shares any accommodation with the landlord and the landlord occupies the premises as his or her only or principal home.

- The occupier shares any of the accommodation with a member of the landlords family, that person occupies the premises as their only or principal home, and the landlord occupies as his or her only or principal home premises in the same building.

- The tenancy or licence was granted temporarily to an occupier who entered the premises as a trespasser.

- The tenancy or licence gives the right to occupy for the purposes of a holiday.

- The tenancy or licence is rent-free.

- The licence relates to occupation of a hostel.

There is also a section in the 1977 Protection from Eviction Act which provides a defense for otherwise unlawful eviction and that is that the landlord may repossess if it is thought that the tenant no longer lives on the premises. It is important to note that, in order for such action to be seen as a crime under the 1977 Protection from Eviction Act, the intention of the landlord to evict must be proved.

However, there is another offence, namely harassment, which also needs to be proved. Even if the landlord is not guilty of permanently depriving a tenant of their home he/she could be guilty of harassment.

Such actions as cutting off services, deliberately allowing the premises to fall into a state of disrepair, or even forcing unwanted sexual attentions, all constitute harassment and a breach of the right to quiet enjoyment.

The 1977 Protection from Eviction Act also prohibits the use of violence to gain entry to premises. Even in situations where the landlord has the right to gain entry without a court order it is an offence to use violence. If entry to the premises is opposed then the landlord should gain a court order.

What can be done against unlawful evictions?

There are two main remedies for unlawful eviction: damages and, as stated above, an injunction.

The injunction

An injunction is an order from the court requiring a person to do, or not to do something. In the case of eviction the court can grant an injunction requiring the landlord to allow a tenant back into occupation of the premises. In the case of harassment an order can be made preventing the landlord from harassing the tenant.

Failure to comply with an injunction is contempt of court and can result in a fine or imprisonment.

Damages

In some cases the tenant can press for financial compensation following unlawful eviction. Financial compensation may have to be paid in cases where financial loss has occurred or in cases where personal hardship alone has occurred.

The tenant can also press for special damages, which means that the tenant may recover the definable out-of-pocket expenses. These could be expenses arising as a result of having to stay in a hotel because of the eviction. Receipts must be kept in that case. There are also general damages, which can be awarded in compensation for stress, suffering and inconvenience. A tenant may also seek exemplary damages where it can be proved that the landlord has disregarded the law deliberately with the intention of making a profit out of the displacement of the tenant.

Now read the main points from chapter Eleven overleaf.

Main points from chapter Eleven

- **Quiet enjoyment.** A tenant has the right to quiet enjoyment of his/her home.

- **Eviction.** It is a criminal offence to unlawfully evict a tenant from his or her home.

- **Use of force.** There are certain circumstances in which the landlord can recover possession without a court order but he/she cannot use force to evict a tenant.

- **Tenants rights.** If a tenant is unlawfully evicted, he/she can seek an injunction to force the landlord to let them back into their home. They can also seek damages for harassment and inconvenience.

12

REPAIRS AND IMPROVEMENTS

....

Repairs and improvements generally: The landlord and tenants obligations

Repairs are essential works to keep the property in good order. Improvements and alterations to the property, e.g. the installation of a shower.

As we have seen, most tenancies are periodic, i.e. week-to-week or month-to-month. If a tenancy falls into this category, or is a fixed-term tenancy for less than seven years, and began after October 1961, then a landlord is legally responsible for most major repairs to the flat or house.

If a tenancy began after 15th January 1989 then, in addition to the above responsibility, the landlord is also responsible for repairs to common parts and service fittings.

The area of law dealing with the landlord and tenants repairing obligations is the 1985 Landlord and Tenant Act, section 11.

This section of the Act is known as a covenant and cannot be excluded by informal agreement between landlord and tenant. In other words the landlord is legally responsible whether he or she likes it or not. Parties to a tenancy, however, may make an application to a court mutually to vary or exclude this section.

Example of repairs a landlord is responsible for:
- Leaking roofs and guttering.
- Rotting windows.

- Rising damp.
- Damp walls.
- Faulty electrical wiring.
- Dangerous ceilings and staircases.
- Faulty gas and water pipes.
- Broken water heaters and boilers.
- Broken lavatories, sinks or baths.

In shared housing the landlord must see that shared halls, stairways, kitchens and bathrooms are maintained and kept clean and lit.

Normally, tenants are responsible only for minor repairs, e.g., broken door handles, cupboard doors, etc. Tenants will also be responsible for decorations unless they have been damaged as a result of the landlord's failure to do repair.

A landlord will be responsible for repairs only if the repair has been reported. It is therefore important to report repairs in writing and keep a copy. If the repair is not carried out then action can be taken. Damages can also be claimed.

Compensation can be claimed, with the appropriate amount being the reduction in the value of the premises to the tenant caused by the landlord's failure to repair. If the tenant carries out the repairs then the amount expended will represent the decrease in value.

The tenant does not have the right to withhold rent because of a breach of repairing covenant by the landlord. However, depending on the repair, the landlord will not have a very strong case in court if rent is withheld.

Reporting repairs to landlords

The tenant has to tell the landlord or the person collecting the rent straight away when a repair needs doing. It is advisable that it is in writing, listing the repairs that need to be done.

Once a tenant has reported a repair the landlord must do it within a reasonable period of time. What is reasonable will depend on the nature of the repair. If certain emergency work needs to be done by the council, such as leaking guttering or drains a notice can be served ordering the landlord to do the work within a short time. In exceptional cases if a home cannot be made habitable at reasonable cost the council may declare that the house must no longer be used, in which case the council has a legal duty to re-house a tenant.

If after the council has served notice the landlord still does not do the work, the council can send in its own builder or, in some cases take the landlord to court. A tenant must allow a landlord access to do repairs. The landlord has to give twenty-four hours notice of wishing to gain access.

The tenants rights whilst repairs are being carried out

The landlord must ensure that the repairs are done in an orderly and efficient way with minimum inconvenience to the tenant If the works are disruptive or if property or decorations are damaged the tenant can apply to the court for compensation or, if necessary, for an order to make the landlord behave reasonably.

If the landlord genuinely needs the house empty to do the work he/she can ask the tenant to vacate it and can if necessary get a court order against the tenant.

A written agreement should be drawn up making it clear that the tenant can move back in when the repairs are completed and stating what the arrangements for fuel charges and rent are.

Can the landlord put the rent up after doing repairs?

If there is a service charge for maintenance, the landlord may be able to pass on the cost of the work(s).

Tenants rights to make improvements to a property

Unlike carrying out repairs the tenant will not normally have the right to insist that the landlord make actual alterations to the home. However, a tenant needs the following amenities and the law states that you should have:

- Bath or shower.
- Wash hand basin.
- Hot and cold water at each bath, basin or shower.
- An indoor toilet.

If these amenities do not exist then the tenant can contact the council's Environmental Health Officer. An improvement notice can be served on the landlord ordering him to put the amenity in.

Disabled tenants

If a tenant is disabled he/she may need special items of equipment in the accommodation. The local authority may help in providing and, occasionally, paying for these. The tenant will need to obtain the permission of the landlord. If you require more information then contact the social services department locally.

Shared housing. The position of tenants in shared houses (Houses in Multiple Occupation)

A major change to improve standards of shared housing was introduced in 2006. The parts of the Housing Act 2004 relating to the licensing of HMO's (Houses in Multiple Occupation) and the new Health and Safety rating System for assessing property conditions came into effect on 6rh April 2006.

The Act requires landlords of many HMO's to apply for licences. The HMO's that need to be licensed are those with:

- Three or more storeys, which are
- Occupied by five or more people forming two or more households (i.e. people not related, living together as a couple etc) and
- Which have an element of shared facilities (eg kitchen, bathroom etc)

As far as licensing is concerned, attics and basements are included as storeys if they are used as living accommodation. Previously, HMO's were only defined as houses converted into flats or bedsits, but the new Act widens this definition and many more types of shared houses are now included.

A local authority will have a list of designated properties will have a list of those properties which are designated HMO's and they will need to be licensed.

Usually, landlords will need to apply to a local authority private sector unit for licences. It has been illegal for landlords to manage designated properties without a licence since July 2006.

Landlords will have to complete an application form and pay a fee, the local authority will then assess whether the property is suitable for the number of people the landlord wants to rent it to. In most case, the local authority, their agents, will visit a property to assess facilities and also fire precautions. A decision will then be taken to grant a license.

There is a fee for registration, councils set the fee and the ones shown below are indicative of a southern local authority:

- Shared houses-five sharers landlords first house £640
- Subsequent house £590
- Plus £10 each additional occupier over five

Hostels

- 10 occupiers £690
- 20 occupiers £790
- 50 occupiers £1100
- 75 occupiers £1340

Housing Grants

There are a range of grants and loans available, almost all discretionary and means tested for help and assistance with property improvement. As the grant regime changes periodically, you should check with your local authority as to the current availability.

Disabled Facilities Grant

The only mandatory grant is the Disabled Facilities Grant, given to those in need, which has been assessed by an Occupational Therapist-the grant has a ceiling. Information of which can be obtained from the local authority. As the name suggests it is for those who are disabled and are n need of works which will make the property accessible and usable for disabled people.

Disabled Facilities Assistance

Disabled Facilities Assistance is in the form of interest free loans, repayable on disposal of the property. To qualify for DFA a person must be at least 18 years old and a freeholder or leaseholder with at least 10 years to expiry of lease and authority to do the work. The maximum amount of assistance is £25,000 or 50% of the equity existing at the time of application. There are a number of other conditions related to the actual works. Details can be obtained from the local authority.

Decent Homes Loans Assistance

This is available to homeowners to enable them to bring their property up to the national Decent Homes Standard. Homes meet Decent Homes standard if they meet a set of criteria which is laid down by the government, such as thermal insulation, overall state of repair etc. Details of the standards can be obtained from the local authority. There are a number of property related criteria and as the money offered is a loan then it will be means tested.

Common Parts Loan/ Common Parts Assistance

This help and assistance is available to owner occupiers (leaseholders) to assist them to meet their liabilities towards the cost of major refurbishment of the common parts of buildings containing their flats, where one or more of the key components of the common parts are old and require replacement or major repair, leading to one or more of the flats becoming 'non-decent' as defined in government guidance. Key components include external walls, roof structure and covering, chimneys etc. Common parts loans are administered by a third party and offered at a subsidized interest rate. They are repayable on disposal of the property.

The criteria for Common Part Loans can be obtained from the local authority.

Landlords Major Works Assistance

Local authorities will usually consider assistance to landlords who elect to bring empty properties back into use as accommodation for homeless people. This will involve leasing properties back to the council for a ten-year period. This scheme will depend on the policy of the local authority.

Minor work assistance

Grants are sometimes available to owner-occupiers and tenants for small-scale work for which they have the responsibility. The aim of such grants will be to ensure the person involved achieves the decent homes standard, improves energy efficiency, improves security or to carry out disabled adaptations as an alternative to DFG.

Details of these various grants and the criteria attached to them can be obtained from the local authority.

Energy Innovation Grants

These grants are subject to the availability of funding and are related to the policy of the local authority.

Sanitation health and hygiene

Local authorities have a duty to serve an owner with a notice requiring the provision of a WC when a property has insufficient sanitation,

sanitation meaning toilet waste disposal.

They will also serve notice if it is thought that the existing sanitation is inadequate and is harmful to health or is a nuisance.

Local authorities have similar powers under various Public Health Acts to require owners to put right bad drains and sewers, also food storage facilities and vermin, plus the containing of disease.

The Environmental Health Department, if it considers the problem bad enough will serve a notice requiring the landlord to put the defect right. In certain cases the local authority can actually do the work and require the landlord to pay for it. This is called work in default.

Now read the main points from chapter twelve overleaf.

Main points from chapter twelve

- **Responsibility for repairs**. If a tenancy is periodic or of a fixed term for less than seven years and began after October 1961, a landlord is legally responsible for certain repairs.

- **The law**. The landlord has repairing obligations under the Landlord and Tenant Act 1985, section 11.

- **Tenants responsibility**. Normally, tenants are responsible only for minor internal repairs.

- **Landlords responsibility**. A landlord will only be responsible for a repair if it has been reported.

- **Local authority**. If a landlord does not carry out repairs then the local authority in particular the Environmental Health Department can get involved.

- **Inconvenience**. A tenant has certain rights whilst repairs are being done, particularly for inconvenience.

- **Improvements**. A tenant will not normally have the right to make improvements. However, they are entitled to certain basic amenities, such as a shower or a bath.

- **Disabled**. A disabled tenant may need certain items of equipment in their home. The local authority can advise and assist in this area, even helping with payment.

- **Shared housing**. There are special laws governing housing in multiple occupation (shared housing) particularly in relation to health and safety. The local authority can advise.

- **Local authority grants**. Private tenants may be entitled to a grant to help with work on a property. The local authority will advise on entitlement.

13

REGAINING
POSSESSION OF A PROPERTY

....

Fast-track possession

In normal circumstances, the landlord will have served a section 21 notice on the tenant at the start of the tenancy. This brings the tenancy to an end on the day of expiry, i.e. on the day of expiry of the six month period, or 12 month period, whichever is appropriate. It should be noted that if a landlord takes a deposit from the tenant then every deposit must be registered with the appropriate deposit service before the landlord can serve the s21 notice. It should also be noted that if a section 21 notice is served after the end of the fixed term giving two months notice then the notice should be a section 21 (b). This is important as a service of the incorrect notice can delay proceedings.

On expiry of the notice, if it is the landlord's intention to take possession of the property then the tenants should leave. It is worthwhile writing a letter to the tenants one month before expiry reminding them that they should leave.

In the event of the tenant refusing to leave, then the landlord has to then follow a process termed 'fast track possession'. This entails filling in the appropriate forms (N5B) which can be downloaded from Her Majesty's Court Service Website www.justice.gov.uk.

Assuming that a valid section 21 notice has been served on the tenant, the accelerated possession proceedings can begin and the forms completed and lodged with the court dealing with the area where the property is situated. In order to grant the accelerated possession order the court will require the following:

- The assured shorthold agreement
- The section 21 notice
- Evidence of service of the section 21 notice

The best form of service of the s21 notice is by hand. If you have already served the notice then evidence that the tenant has received it will be required.

Having the correct original paperwork is of the utmost importance. Without this, the application will fail and delays will be incurred.

A copy must also be served on the tenant. This will be done by the court although it might help if the landlord also serves a copy informing the tenant that they are taking proceedings. If the tenant disputes the possession proceedings in any way they will have 14 days to reply to the court. If the case is well founded and the paperwork is in order then there should be no case for defence. Once the accelerated possession order has been granted then this will need to be served on the tenant, giving them 14 days to vacate. In certain circumstances, if the tenant pleads hardship the court can grant extra time to leave, six weeks as opposed to two weeks. If they still do not vacate then an application will need to be made to court for a bailiffs warrant to evict the tenants.

Accelerated possession proceedings cannot be used against the tenant for rent arrears. It will be necessary to follow the procedure below.

An accelerated possession order remains in force for six years from the date it was granted.

Going to court to end the tenancy

There may come a time when you need to go to court to regain possession of your property. This will usually arise when the contract has been breached by the tenant, for non-payment of rent or for some other breach such as nuisance or harassment. As we have seen, a tenancy can be brought to an end in a court on one of the grounds for possession. However, as the tenancy will usually be an assured shorthold then it is necessary to consider whether you are in a position to give two months notice and withhold the deposit, as opposed to going to court. The act of withholding the deposit will entail you refusing to authorize the payment to the tenant online. This then brings arbitration into the frame. Deposit schemes have an arbitration system as an integral part of the scheme.

If you decide, for whatever reason, to go to court, then any move to regain your property for breach of agreement will commence in the county court in the area in which the property is. The first steps in ending the tenancy will necessitate the serving of a notice of seeking possession using one of the Grounds for Possession detailed earlier in the book. If the tenancy is protected then 28 days must be given, the notice must be in prescribed form and served on the tenant personally (preferably).

If the tenancy is an assured shorthold, which is more often the case now, then 14 days notice of seeking possession can be used. In all cases the ground to be relied upon must be clearly outlined in the notice. If the case is more complex, then this will entail a particulars of claim being prepared, usually by a solicitor, as opposed to a standard possession form.

A fee is paid when sending the particulars to court, which should be checked with the local county court. The standard form which the landlord uses for routine rent arrears cases is called the N119 and the accompanying summons is called the N5. Both of these forms can be obtained from the court or from www.courtservice.gov. When completed, the forms should be sent in duplicate to the county court and a copy retained for you.

The court will send a copy of the particulars of claim and the summons to the tenant. They will send you a form which gives you a case number and court date to appear, known as the return date.

On the return date, you should arrive at court at least 15 minutes early. You can represent yourself in simple cases but are advised to use a solicitor for more contentious cases.

When it is your turn to present the case, you should have your file in order, a copy of all relevant notices served and a current rent arrears figure or a copy of the particulars for other cases. If it is simple rent arrears then quite often the judge will guide you through. However, the following are the steps to observe:

- State your name and address.
- Tenants name and address.
- Start date of tenancy.
- Current rent and arrears.
- Date notice served-a copy should be produced for the judge.
- Circumstances of tenant (financial and other) this is where you make your case.
- Copy of order wanted.

If the tenant is present then they will have a chance to defend themselves.

A number of orders are available. However, if you have gone to court on the mandatory ground eight then if the fact is proved then you will get possession immediately. If not, then the judge can grant an order, suspended whilst the tenant finds time to pay.

In a lot of cases, it is more expedient for a landlord to serve notice-requiring possession, if the tenancy has reached the end of the period, and then wait two months before the property is regained. This saves the cost and time of going to court particularly if the ground is one of nuisance or other, which will involve solicitors.

In many cases, if you are contemplating going to court and have never been before and do not know the procedure then it is best to use a solicitor to guide the case through. Costs can be recovered from the tenant, although this depends on the tenant's means.

If you regain possession of your property midway through the contractual term then you will have to complete the possession process by use of bailiff, pay a fee and fill in another form, Warrant for Possession of Land.

If you have reached the end of the contractual term and wish to recover your property then a fast track procedure is available which entails gaining an order for possession and bailiff's order by post. This can be used in cases with the exception of rent arrears.

Now read the main points from chapter thirteen.

Main points from chapter thirteen

- One of the unpleasant sides of being a landlord is that you may have to go to court to regain possession of a property.

- Any move to regain possession of your property will commence in the local county court where the property is. Fourteen days service of notice is needed and a fee is payable to the court. It is usually best to employ a solicitor to take this action.

- In many cases it is better to serve a section 21 notice and regain possession either at the end of the fixed term or after two months from service rather than incur the expense of court action.

14

INCOME TAX AND PROPERTY MANAGEMENT

....

Income tax and property

Anyone investing in property is liable to pay income tax on any profitable income earned from their properties. There are two main categories of people who invest in property, the property investor and the property trader/ dealer. This book deals mainly with the property investor, the person who lets out property for profit.

The investor

The investor will usually invest for the long term and let those properties out for a rental return. Income tax is due on that return, minus tax deductible items, which we will be discussing shortly.

The property trader/ dealer

Property traders or dealers will invest in a property for the short term and will sell on quickly making a profit. Property dealers and traders will pay income tax on proceeds of sale

See overleaf for current income tax rates.

Income tax bands 2011/2012

INCOME TAX 2011-2012			
RATE/ALLOWANCE	RATE	BAND	GENERAL
SINGLE-PERSON ALLOWANCE	NIL	£0 TO 35,000	THE FIRST £7,475 OF EACH INDIVIDUALS INCOME IS TAX FREE
BASIC RATE	20%	£7,475 TO £35,000	
HIGHER RATE	40%	£35,400 to 150,000	ANY INCOME ABOVE £35,000 WILL BE TAXED AT 40%.
Additional rate	50%	Over £150,000	

Case study for tax calculations
1. Basic income tax calculation for landlords

Basic rate taxpayer

The examples below relate to the 2010-2011 tax years.

Fred works for a local factory and receives an annual salary of £20,000. He decides to invest in a property for which he pays £120,000. He rents this out for £600 per month. He receives an annual income of £7,200 as the property is let out for the whole of the tax year (2010/11). In the tax year he has incurred property related expenses of £3225, as follows:

Interest on mortgage: £1800

Maintenance: £800

Safety checks (mandatory) £125

Central heating contract £250

Other small maintenance items £300

Total £3225

This means that the taxable profit is £7200-£3225 =£3975

On this amount he is liable to pay tax at 20% on the rental (2010-2011) profit of £3975. His tax liability therefore will be £795.

All tax liabilities should be worked out on this same basic principle but utilising the correct tax band.

CHARGES
Offsetting interest charges

Whether or not interest payments or mortgages or other types of loan can be offset against a mortgage will very much depend on the type of loan.

Interest on mortgages

This is the most common type of interest that is associated with property investors. This interest relates specifically to the amount you pay back to your mortgage lender that is above and beyond the initial amount borrowed. It doesn't matter whether the mortgage is interest only or repayment, the fact that you are making interest payments means that they can be offset.

Interest on personal loans

If you take out a personal loan that is used wholly and exclusively for the purpose of the property then the interest charged on this loan can also be offset. The following are typical situations when interest charged on a personal loan can be offset:

- Loans used for providing a deposit on a property. In this situation, for example, if a 20% deposit is raised by way of a loan then the interest on the loan plus the mortgage can be claimed back.

- Loans used for refurbishments or developments. If a property needs refurbishment or redevelopment, which many do at certain stages in their life, then the interest on this type of loan can be offset.

Although the general rule is that interest payable on a loan not used for a property is not claimable, paragraph 45700 of HMRC Business Income Manual gives landlords the opportunity to release equity from their investment properties and offset the interest due from the equity release regardless of what the money has been used for. The only restriction is that the equity release cannot be greater than the market value of the property when it was brought into the property business. For more information on this you should contact HMRC.

Wear and tear and renewals-relief from income tax

There are two important methods which can be utilised to reduce your income tax bill:

- The 10% wear and tear allowance

- The renewals basis method

The above both relate to furnishings provided in your property. Choosing the right one can have a significant impact on your final tax bill.

The 10% Wear and Tear Allowance

This is an allowance that HMRC has introduced. It allows you to offset 10% of your annual rental income against tax. There are some important points to note:

1) HMRC state that:

The Wear and tear Allowance is calculated by taking 10% of the net rental income received for the furnished residential accommodation. To find the 'net rent' you deduct charges and services that would normally be borne by a tenant but are, in fact, borne by you (e.g. council tax, water , sewerage etc).
It doesn't matter how much you spend on furnishing you can only offset 10% of your net rental income.
The 10% Wear and tear Allowance can only be claimed when the property is furnished

.

HMRC's definition of a furnished property is as follows:
'A furnished property is one which is capable of normal occupation without the tenant having to provide their own beds, chairs, tables, sofas and other furnishings, cooker etc.'
The 10% Wear and Tear Allowance cannot be used for partly furnished or unfurnished properties.

The Renewals Basis method

The renewals basis method is calculated differently from the Wear and Tear allowance and can be used for a furnished, partly furnished, or even an unfurnished property.

The renewals method allows you to offset the cost of renewing or replacing an item in a property. Unlike the 10% Wear and Tear Allowance there are no restrictions as to when this rule can be used. As usual, with HMRC, there are important points to note:

a) The initial cost of an item cannot be offset. You can only offset when renewing.

b) If you use this allowance, then you cannot change between this method and the Wear and Tear Allowance on a weekly basis.

If you decide to replace an item and receive some income from selling the old one then this amount must be taken into account when calculating tax liability.

Maintenance and repairs to a property

The basic rule here is that any maintenance costs incurred that help prevent the property from deteriorating can be offset against rental income. Maintenance costs cannot be claimed if they constitute a capital improvement, i.e. they result in an increase in the value of your property. The following are typical maintenance and repair costs which can be offset:

• Repairing water or gas leaks and burst pipes etc;

- Electrical faults;

- Broken windows, doors, guttering, roof tiles etc;

- Repairs to walls, roof, etc;

- Painting and redecorating the property;

- Treatment for damp or dry rot;

- Re-pointing the brickwork;

- Hiring equipment needed in carrying out the repair work;

- Repairing existing fixtures and fittings which include radiators, boilers, water tanks and so on.

Capital improvements

As stated, capital improvements to properties cannot be offset against rental income. This is simply because it is not classed as maintenance or repair work. However, this cost can be offset against any capital gain made when selling the property. (see further on in this section-Capital Gains)

Replacing fixtures and fittings

Fixtures and fittings are classed as items that are an integral part of the property. Examples include:
- Windows, doors and light fittings;

- Kitchen units;

- Bathroom suites;

- Gas central heating systems and radiators or hot water supply tanks;

- Gas fires etc.

The most important point to understand about fixtures and fittings is that any cost incurred in repairing them or replacing them with a like-for-like product can be offset against the rental income. This is regardless of the furnished status of the property. Two important conditions must be satisfied before you can offset the cost of replacing fixtures and fittings:

- The cost must be a 'replacement' cost. It cannot be for the installation of fixtures and fittings that were not previously in the property;

- The cost must be for a similar 'like-for-like product.

If the above conditions are met then the costs can be deducted from the rental profits. Whenever you decide to replace existing fixtures and fittings, they are likely to fall into one of the below three categories:

- Like-for-like replacement;

- Like-for like replacement but with capital improvement;

- Replacement with superior fixtures and fittings.

Each of the above is treated differently with regards to calculating your tax bill.

If you replace like-for-like then the whole amount is reclaimable. In some circumstances it is not possible to replace with like-for like. This is understood and appreciated by HMRC and in such circumstances it is possible to replace with a superior item as long as the cost differential is not too great.

If you replace the existing fixtures and fittings with a like-for-like product but also make a capital improvement as well, then you can only offset the cost of the like-for-like replacement.

Other costs that can be offset are:

Rents Rates and Insurance

The following costs are incurred by property investors when the property is let or in between lets and empty:

Rents
The most common type of rent that an investor is likely to incur is that of ground rent, which will typically be incurred on a leasehold property.

Rates
The following can be offset:

- Water;

- Electricity;

- Gas;

- Council tax;

- Service charges;

- TV licence;

- Telephone line rental;

- Satellite TV charges etc.

Insurance

Any insurance premiums that are paid relating to the property or products and services can be offset against income. The most common are buildings insurance, contents insurance and insurance for appliances.

Offsetting pre-trading expenditure

These are expenses incurred in the seven years before commencement of a rental business, expenses such as travel costs, telephone calls etc. However, be very careful here as HMRC scrutinises such claims carefully.

Carrying over rental losses

Any rental losses made on a property can be carried forward into the next financial year.

Travelling costs

It is likely that anyone with a property to let will incur travelling costs to and from that property. There are two methods of claiming travel costs:

Car usage

You can claim the cost of travel to and from the property as long as the trip was wholly for a business purpose. This is normally done using the 'apportionment method'. The apportionment method involves keeping a log of the annual car mileage and all the expenditure that has been incurred on the car., including petrol receipts. You then determine how many miles were used in connection with the property business and apportion accordingly.

Public transport

If you use public transport to travel to your property, then you can offset the cost as long as the trip is wholly and exclusively for the purpose of the property.

Overseas property

A lot of investors now own property overseas. The cost of going to look at a potential overseas investment cannot be offset against UK rental income. This is a hard and fast rule.

Multiple properties

If you have numerous properties then it may not always be possible to attribute costs to individual properties, such as decorating costs. In this case you should use the apportionment method.

Storage costs

Many landlords will incur storage costs. The cost of renting storage space is allowable against rental income, a song as the space is wholly and exclusively for the purpose of the property business.

Other general costs that can be offset

The following are general costs that can be offset:

- Gas and electrical safety;

- Stationary;

- Computer equipment;

- Bad debts;

- Legal and professional costs;

- Service costs;

- Advertising costs;

- Letting agents costs;

- Books, magazines and so on;

- Telephone calls (itemised);

- Bank charges.

Training courses, such as seminars, as long as they are incurred wholly and exclusively for the purpose of the business within which the landlord operates, and the landlord is already a property investor, are allowable. The important phrase here is 'already a property investor'. A person cannot claim for a property seminar if, for example, they are thinking about a career change but are not already an investor.

Capital allowances for landlords

A 25% depreciation allowance can be claimed if you decide to purchase a piece of equipment or an asset for the purpose of the business. Examples of such assets include:

- Computers and office furniture

- Tools for maintaining upkeep of properties

- Vehicles (subject to restrictions-this is restricted to the lower of the unrelieved balance or £3000)

The depreciation allowance can be claimed annually until the equipment/asset is disposed of.

Property rental income profit calculation

There are two methods that can be used to calculate your annual UK property income tax. These methods are known as 'Cash Basis' and 'Earnings Basis'.

Cash Basis

The cash basis can be used when the income generated from your property rental business (before other allowable business expenses are deducted) does not exceed £15,000 in the tax year.

When the cash basis is used, the income tax calculation is based on when the rent was actually *received* and when the expenditures were *paid.* HMRC accept this basis of calculating when the cash basis is 'small' not exceeding £15,000 per year and when it is consistently used.

Earnings basis

The earnings basis is also referred to as the 'accruals' method and follows ordinary commercial accounting rules. This is the usual method used by accountants. If the rental income is above £15,000 per annum then this method must be used.

CAPITAL GAINS TAX

Many property investors find the issue of capital gains tax a problem, especially when it is time to sell properties, for whatever reason.

It should be noted that after June 2010 new capital gains tax rates apply and you should contact HMRC for these rates.

There are two main Capital Gains Tax savings reliefs that are available to investors. These are known as the 36-month rule and the Private Residence relief.

The 36-month rule

Provided that a house has at some time been your main residence, the last three years of ownership are always treated as though you lived there. This is the case even if you didn't actually live there in those last three years. Over the last three years, numerous property investors who know about this tax relief have bought new property but retained and let out their existing property. The case study below will illustrate this point.

The 36-month Rule to get relief

Fred buys an apartment in South London for £150,000 in 1995. He lives in his apartment for eight years before deciding to move in with his girlfriend in 2003. He rents his apartment out for three years before deciding to sell it in 2006, which he does for £275,000. He has no capital gains tax on the profit of £125,000 because for the first eight years he lived there. He also has no capital gain on the three rental years as he is able to claim the 36 month rule, which means that the last 36 months of ownership are exempt from CGT.

A further case study below illustrates the effect of using the 36 month rule to obtain partial residence relief.

Instead of selling his property after 3 years Fred keeps it for another three years and sells it in 2009 (no credit crunch in this fictional world) for £325,000, realising a profit of £175,000. Having lived there for eight years and rented it out for six years (14 in total) Fred can claim eight years as his residence and three years through the 36 month rule. He therefore will only be liable to pay 3/14 of the profit as a CGT.

If you have invested in property and let it out as soon as you have brought it, you can still benefit from the 36 month rule. All you need to do is to make it your principal private residence before you sell it. You do not need to live in a property before you let it out to claim the 36-month rule.

Using private residence relief to avoid CGT

If you still have a taxable capital gain after using the 36-month rue, then it is possible that any tax liability can be eliminated by using the **private residence relief.**

HMRC state that a private residence relief can be used where:

- You sell a dwelling house which is, or has been, your only or main residence, and

- Part or all of it has at some time in your period of ownership been let as a residential accommodation.

The amount of private residence relief that can be claimed cannot be greater than £40,000 and it must be the lowest of the following three values:

- £40,000;

- The amount of private residence relief that has already been claimed;

- The amount of any chargeable gain that is made due to the letting; that is, this is the amount that is attributed to the increase in the property value during the period that it was let.

The use of this relief is illustrated in the following case study.

Private Residence Relief

Fred buys a five-bed house in Cornwall in 1995 for £70,000. He lives in the house for two years then moves and rents it out for the next five years. In 2002 he sells the house in Cornwall for £140,000. This means that he has made a capital gain of £70,000. Five sevenths of the profit will be exempt from CGT because Fred is able to claim partial residence relief (two years PPR and the 36-month rule). This means that he will only have to pay CGT on the remaining £20,000. However, Fred is also able to claim private residence relief and the amount that he can claim is the lower of the below three values:

- £40,000;

- Amount of private residence relief already claimed is £50,000;

- Amount of any chargeable gain that is made due to the letting is £20,000 (assuming that the property increased by £10,000 per year in each of the two years that the property was let.

This means that Fred can claim private residence relief of £20,000 as this is the lower of the three values.

Therefore the outstanding chargeable gain is cancelled out by this relief which means that there is no CGT liability.

It is realised that the above can be quite confusing. Not all accountants have an accurate grasp of property taxation. It is recommended that you seek advice from an experienced property accountant as the above is for guidance only.

Also, as discussed it is likely that there will be a change in the financial regime relating to CGT very soon.

Now read the main points from chapter fourteen overleaf

Main points from chapter fourteen

- Anyone investing in property is liable to pay income tax

- There are two main categories of people who invest in property- the investor and the trader

- Relevant interest charges can be set off against income

- Renewals and wear and tear can be offset

- Certain maintenance costs-disregarding improvements can be offset against income

- Other charges such as rents, rates and insurance can be offset

- Capital gains tax is payable although can be minimized subject to HMRC rules

15

PRIVATE TENANCIES IN SCOTLAND

The law governing the relationship between private landlords and tenants in Scotland is different to that in England. Since the beginning of 1989, new private sector tenancies in Scotland have been covered by the Housing (Scotland) Act 1988. Following the passage of this Act, private sector tenants no longer have any protection as far as rent levels are concerned and tenants enjoy less security of tenure.

There are four essential elements in the creation of a tenancy under Scottish law:

- An agreement between landlord and tenant.
- The payment of rent. If someone is allowed to occupy a property without an agreement then this will not amount to a tenancy.
- A fixed permission date (called an 'ish').
- Possession.

The agreement must be in writing if the tenancy is for a period of 1 year or more. Agreements of less than a year can be oral.

Different types of tenancy

There are different tenancy types in the private sector, differing according to when they were entered into. In the case of assured tenancies they will differ depending on what landlord and tenant agreed between themselves. The different types of tenancy are:

- Protected tenancy.
- Statutory tenancy.
- Assured tenancy.
- Short assured tenancy.

Protected tenancies

Before 1989, most private sector tenancies were likely to be protected tenancies. A protected tenancy is a contractual tenancy covered by the Rent Act (Scotland) 1984 and must satisfy the following requirements:

- The house must be let as a dwelling house (this can apply to a house or part of a house).
- The house must be a separate dwelling.
- The ratable value must be less than a specified sum.

Various categories of dwellings did not qualify as protected tenancies. A protected tenancy retains its status until the death of a tenant or his spouse, or any eligible successor, and therefore some protected tenancies are still in existence today.

Grounds for possession

As is the case in England and Wales, where there is no protected tenancy, the landlord may possess a property only by obtaining a court order. The landlord must serve a notice to quit, giving 28 days notice. A ground for possession must be shown, either discretionary or mandatory before possession can be given. The grounds for possession are similar to those in England and Wales, with ten mandatory and ten discretionary grounds applying.

Fair rent system

A fair rent system, similar to England and Wales, exists in Scotland for protected tenants. There is a set procedure to be followed, with either the landlord or tenant, or jointly, making an application to the rent officer. Once fixed, the rent is valid for three years. A fresh application can be made within three years if circumstances relating to the tenancy radically alter, such as a substantial refurbishment.

Statutory tenancies

A statutory tenancy is one which arises when a tenant remains in possession of a house after the contractual tenancy has been terminated (e.g. by a notice to quit) or a tenant has previously succeeded to the tenancy before 1990. A statutory tenant has similar rights to a protected tenant.

Assured tenants

Under the Housing (Scotland) Act 1988, the assured tenancy was introduced into Scotland coming into force after 2nd January 1989. This is very similar indeed to the assured tenancy introduced into England and Wales in 1989.

A Scottish assured tenancy has three elements:

- The tenancy must be of a house or flat or self contained dwelling. For an agreement to exist, there must be an agreement, rent payable, a termination date and possession, as there is in all leases in Scotland.
- The house must be let as a separate dwelling. A tenancy may be of a flat, part of a house, or even a single room, provided it is possible for

the tenant to carry on all 'the major activities of residential life there, i.e. sleeping, cooking and feeding.

- The tenant must be an individual. A company cannot be given an assured tenancy.

The list of exclusions from assured tenancy status are the same as those in England and all the other provisions concerning rent, sub-letting succession, security of tenure and so on, apply.

The grounds for possession and the law governing termination of tenancies is a reflection of English Law.

Short-assured tenancies

The Housing Act (Scotland) also introduced 'short assured tenancies', a distinct form of assured tenancy for a fixed term of six months. Again, this is a reflection of the assured shorthold with the same provisions applying. The short assured tenant has little security of tenure. See appendix for an example of tenancy and notice (AT5) which must be served on the tenant prior to entering into the agreement stating that the agreement is a short assured tenancy. The following are the conditions for the creation of a short assured tenancy:

- The tenancy fulfills the requirements of a valid assured tenancy.
- The landlord, before the creation of the tenancy, has served on the tenant a formal notice (AT5) stating that the proposed tenancy is to be a short assured. tenancy and giving various information set out in regulations.
- The tenancy is for a fixed period of not less than six-months (there is no maximum period).

Private Tenancies in Scotland

One main difference between assured shorthold tenancies and short assured is that, if neither landlord nor tenant take any action to renew the tenancy at the end of the fixed period (6 months) then the tenancy will automatically renew for the same minimum fixed period (or one year if the fixed period was more than one year). This is known as tacit relocation.

Recovery of possession

A short assured tenant has no defence to a properly based possession action. The sheriff must grant an order for possession if he is satisfied that all of the following apply:

- The tenancy has reached its termination date.
- No tacit relocation is in action (i.e. a valid notice to quit of at least 40 days has been served by the landlord.
- No further contractual tenancy is in existence.
- The landlord has given at least two months notice to the tenant that he requires possession of the house. The notice can be served during the tenancy or after the termination date.

As with the English Assured shorthold, the landlord does not need to give any reason why he needs possession. In addition, because the short assured tenancy is a type of assured tenancy then recovery using the grounds for possession is the same as the assured tenancy. It can be seen that, apart from a number of minor differences, there are many similarities between the assured shorthold and the short assured tenancy.

Now read the main points from chapter fifteen.

135

Main points from Chapter fifteen

- Private sector tenancies in Scotland are regulated by the Housing (Scotland) Act 1988.

- Agreements of 1 year or more must be in writing. Agreements for less than 1 year can be verbal.

- The most common form of private sector tenancy is the short assured tenancy.

- There are many similarities between the short assured tenancy and the assured shorthold tenancy.

16

ADVICE FOR TENANTS

....

Although this guide is aimed at landlords, or prospective landlords, it is important not to forget the tenant, the person who makes rental investments possible. The relationship between landlord and tenant is not based solely on the law but is also based on common decency and understanding. Landlords will also find the following advice useful when contemplating letting out properties.

If you are a tenant viewing prospective apartments it is important to understand that the property, unless otherwise stated, is 'as seen'. Generally speaking, items that are not included in an inventory are not available to the tenant.

Once you have chosen the property that you want to make your home, the next step is to provide the landlord or agent with satisfactory references. Most agencies will require references from your bank, a previous landlord or agent and a personal reference usually from an employer. These will be applied for directly so they cannot be faked.

Some agencies use a credit reference agency for this purpose and there may be a charge for this.

Guarantees

In some cases, particularly if the tenant is on benefits, the landlord will require rental payment guarantees, and this involves getting someone to act as a guarantor. This will be someone who is prepared to stand as guarantor for the rent for the entire duration of the tenancy, including any renewals and extensions. For many tenants this has proved a sticking point as it is quite a lot to ask anyone.

However, provided that both you and the references are suitable, and any guarantees are in place, the next step will be to draw up a tenancy agreement. This should be read very thoroughly including the small print. Do not sign anything that you are not happy with.

Once the agreement has been entered into it is returned to the landlord or agent with a holding deposit of (usually) £200 to secure the tenancy which is deducted from the final amount handed over.

Before the tenancy commences. You will receive an invoice detailing all monies to be paid over before you take possession. These include:

- The initial rent, usually one month, depending on the terms of the agreement.
- The deposit, which will usually be one months rent. The deposit covers dilapidations and damage. This is registered by the landlord with one of three agencies which were set up in April 2007 in order to protect tenants deposits. See previous chapters.
- The inventory contribution fee. Usually, unless the tenant is a company, the landlord will pay for the inventory.
- The credit reference fee if applicable.
- The tenancy agreement fee. This is non-refundable should you, for any reason, decide not to proceed with the tenancy. Most agencies will only charge the tenant for the agreement if it deviates in important ways from the assured shorthold agreement, i.e. if the tenancy is for a short let, if it is for a company let, or if the rent exceeds a certain figure per annum which puts it outside an assured shorthold.

On the day the tenancy commences the landlord or agent will check you into the property, you will need to sign a form as to the condition of the property. Meter readings should be taken at the check in and the landlord or agent concerned will notify the various utilities companies of the change. Sometimes this does not happen and it is important that the tenant does this.

Remember, your landlord is responsible for most repairs and it is important that you notify him or the agent immediately when there is a problem. The landlord is only responsible once notified of a problem.

Useful websites

The Buying Process
The Local Government Association
www.Iga.gov.uk
Confederation of Scottish Local Authorities
www.cosla.gov.uk
Greater London Authority
www.london.gov.uk
The Environment Agency
www.environment-agency.gov.uk
www.homecheckuk.com

House Prices
Halifax www.halifax.co.uk
Nationwide www.nationwide.co.uk
Land Registry www.landreg.gov.uk
www.zoopla.co.uk
www.ourproperty.co.uk
www.upmystreet.com

Property search sites
www.hometrack.co.uk
www.rightmove.co.uk
www.zoopla.co.uk
www.fish4.co.uk
www.findaproperty.com
www.thisislondon.co.uk

The buying and selling process
The Law Society www.lawsoc.org.uk
The Council of Mortgage Lenders www.cml.org.uk
HM Customs and Revenue www.hmrc.gov

Scotland
Law Society of Scotland www.scotlaw.org.uk

Leasehold/freehold
Lease www.lease-advice.org
Association of Residential Managing Agents
www.arma.org.uk

Mortgage search sites/brokers
Money facts www.moneyfacts.co.uk
www.moneysupermarket.co.uk
www.moneynet.co.uk

New homes
NHBC www.nhbc.co.uk

Renting and Letting
Association of Residential Letting Agencies (ARLA)
ARLA Administration
Maple House
53-55 Woodside Road
Amersham
Bucks
HP6 6AA
Tel: 01923 896555

Website: www.arla.co.uk
Email: info@arla.co.uk

Specialist rental property sites

www.zoopla.co.uk
www.rightmove.co.uk

Auctions
www.propwatch.com
www.primelocation.com
www.bbc.co.uk/homes/property/buying_auction
www.propertyauctions.com
www.netguide.co.uk/Buying_A_House_At_Auction

A SUMMARY OF IMPORTANT TERMS

FREEHOLDER: Someone who owns their property outright.

LEASEHOLDER: Someone who has been granted permission to live on someone else's land for a fixed term.

TENANCY: One form of lease, the most common types of which are fixed-term or periodic.

LANDLORD: A person who owns the property in which the tenant lives.

LICENCE: A licence is an agreement entered into whereby the landlord is merely giving you permission to occupy his/her property for a limited period of time.

TRESPASSER: Someone who has no right through an agreement to live in a property.

PROTECTED TENANT: In the main, subject to certain exclusions, someone whose tenancy began before 15th January 1989.

ASSURED TENANT: In the main, subject to certain exclusions, someone whose tenancy began after 15th January 1989.

NOTICE TO QUIT: A legal document giving the protected tenant twenty eight days notice that the landlord intends to apply for possession of the property to the County Court.

GROUND FOR POSSESSION: One of the stated reasons for which the landlord can apply for possession of the property.

MANDATORY GROUND: Where the judge must give possession of the property.

DISCRETIONARY GROUND: Where the judge may or may not give possession, depending on his own opinion.

STUDENT LETTING: A tenancy granted by a specified educational institution.

HOLIDAY LETTING: A dwelling used for holiday purposes only.

ASSURED SHORTHOLD TENANCY: A fixed-term post-1989 tenancy.

PAYMENT OF RENT: Where you pay a regular sum of money in return for permission to occupy a property or land for a specified period of time.

FAIR RENT: A rent set by the Rent Officer every two years for most pre-1989 tenancies and is lower than a market rent.

MARKET RENT: A rent deemed to be comparable with other non-fair rents in the area.

RENT ASSESSMENT COMMITTEE: A committee set up to review rents set by either the Rent Officer or the landlord.

PREMIUM: A sum of money charged for permission to live in a property.

DEPOSIT: A sum of money held against the possibility of damage to property.

QUIET ENJOYMENT: The right to live peacefully in your own home.

REPAIRS: Work required to keep a property in good order.

IMPROVEMENTS: Alterations to a property.

LEGAL AID: Help with your legal costs, which is dependent on income.

HOUSING BENEFIT: Financial help with rent, which is dependent on income.

HOUSING ADVICE CENTRE: A center which exists to give advice on housing-related matters and which is usually local authority-funded.

LAW CENTRE: A center, which exists for the purpose of assisting the public with legal advice.

Index

Appendix 1

Sample Assured Shorthold Tenancy Agreement (England and Wales)

Sample Section 21 Notice Requiring possession

Sample Notices Scotland

Sample Landlords Inventory

Appendices

1. Sample Assured Shorthold Tenancy Agreement
2. Sample Section 21 Notice Requiring Possession
3. Landlords notice to Terminate (Scotland)
4. Notice to Quit Scotland
5. Example Inventory

ASSURED SHORTHOLD TENANCY AGREEMENT
ENGLAND AND WALES

This Tenancy Agreement is between

Name and address of Landlord-
-AND

Name of tenant:

he Tenant"

(in the case of Joint Tenants the term "Tenant" applies to each of them and the names of all Joint Tenants should be written above. Each Tenant individually has the full responsibilities and rights set out in this Agreement)

Address-in respect of:

("the Premises")

Description of Premises
-Which comprises of:
Term-The Tenancy is granted for a fixed term of [6] months

Date of start of tenancy-The Tenancy begins on:

("The Commencement Date") and is an assured shorthold monthly tenancy, the terms of which are set out in this Agreement.

Overcrowding-The Tenant agrees not to allow any person other than the Tenant to reside at the Premises.

Payment of Deposit-The Tenant agrees to pay on signing the Agreement a deposit of £ which will be returnable in full providing that the Landlord may deduct from such sums: The reasonable costs of any necessary repairs to the premises, building or common parts, or the replacement of any or all of the contents where such repair or replacement is due to any act or omission of the Tenant or family or visitors of the Tenant, such sums as are outstanding on leaving the Premises in respect of arrears or other charges including Court costs or other fees.

The deposit will be protected by The Deposit Protection Service (The DPS) in accordance with the Terms and Conditions of The DPS. The Terms and Conditions and ADR Rules governing the protection of the deposit including the repayment process can be found at www.depositprotection.com

Payment for the premises-
Rent: The rent for the premises is:
            Service Charge:
            Total:

In this Agreement the term "Rent" refers to the net rent and service charge set out above or as varied from time to time in accordance with this Agreement. The payment of monthly Rent is due in advance on the first Saturday of each month.

The service charge is in respect of the landlord providing the services listed in Schedule 1 to this Agreement for which the Tenant shall pay a service charge to be included in the rent. The service charge may be varied by the landlord in accordance with the terms set out in Schedule 1 to this Agreement.

I/We have read, understood and accept the terms and conditions contained within this agreement which include the standard terms and conditions attached.

Signed by the Tenant

.... Dated:

Signed on behalf of the landlord

.... Dated:

If the Tenant feels that the landlord has broken this Agreement or not performed any obligation contained in it, he/she should first complain to the landlord in writing giving details of the breach or non-performance.

Terms and Conditions

1. It is agreed that:

Changes in Rent-1.1-The landlord may increase or decrease the Rent by giving the Tenant not less than 4 weeks notice in writing of the increase or decrease. The notice shall specify the Rent proposed. The first increase or decrease shall be on the first day of   following the Commencement Date of this Agreement. Subsequent increases or decreases in the Rent shall take effect on the first day of   in each subsequent year. The revised Rent shall be the amount specified in the notice of increase unless the Tenant exercises his/her right to refer the notice to a Rent Assessment Committee to have a market rent determined in which case the maximum Rent payable for one year after the date specified in the notice shall be the Rent so determined.

Altering the Agreement-1.2-With the exception of any changes in Rent, this Agreement may only be altered by the agreement in writing of both the Tenant and the landlord.

2. The landlord agrees:

Possession-2.1-To give the Tenant possession of the Premises at the commencement of the Tenancy.

Tenant's Right to Occupy-2.2-Not to interrupt or interfere with the Tenant's right peacefully to occupy the Premises except where:

(i)   access is required to inspect the condition of the Premises or to carry out repairs or other works to the Premises or adjoining property; or

(ii)   a court has given the Association possession by ending the Tenancy.

Repair of Structure and Exterior-2.3-To keep in good repair the structure and exterior of the Premises including:

(i)   drains, gutters and external pipes;

(ii)   the roof;

(iii)   outside wall, outside doors, windowsills, window catches, sash cords and window frames including necessary external painting and decorating;

(iv)   internal walls, floors and ceilings, doors and door frames, door hinges and skirting boards but not including internal painting and decoration;

(v)   plasterwork;

(vi)   chimneys, chimney stacks and flues but not including sweeping;

(vii)   pathways, steps or other means of access;

(viii) integral garages and stores;

(ix)   boundary walls and fences.

Repair of Installations-2.4-To keep in good repair and working order any installations provided by the landlord for space heating, water heating and sanitation and for the supply of water, gas and electricity including:

(i)   basins, sinks, baths, toilets, flushing systems and waste pipes;

(ii)   electric wiring including sockets and switches, gas pipes and water pipes;

(iii)   water heaters, fireplaces, fitted fires and central heating installations

Repair of Common Parts-2.5-To take reasonable care to keep the common entrances, halls, stairways, lifts, passageways, rubbish chutes and any other common parts, including their lighting, in reasonable repair and fit for use by the Tenant and other occupiers and visitors to the Premises.

External & Internal
Decorations-2.6-To keep the exterior and interior of the Premises and any common parts in a good state of decoration and normally to decorate these areas once every 5 years.

3. The Tenant agrees:

Possession-3.1-To take possession of the Premises at the commencement of the Tenancy and not to part with possession of the Premises or sub-let the whole or part of it.

Rent-3.2-To pay the Rent monthly and in advance. The first payment shall be made on the signing of the Agreement in respect of the period from the Commencement Date to the first Saturday of the following month.

Use of Premises-3.3-To use the Premises for residential purposes as the Tenant's only or principal home and not to operate a business at the Premises without the written consent of the landlord.

Nuisance and Racial and other Harassment-3.4-Not to behave or allow members of his/her household or any other person visiting the Premises with the Tenant's permission to behave in a manner nor do anything which is likely to be a nuisance to the tenants, owners or lessees of any of the other properties or other persons lawfully visiting the property. In particular, not to cause any interference, nuisance or annoyance through noise, anti-social behaviour or threats of or actual violence or any damage to property belonging to the said persons. This Clause also applies to any conduct or activity which amounts to harassment including: abuse and intimidation, creating unacceptable levels of noise or causing intentional damage or any other persistent behaviour which causes offence, discomfort or inconvenience on the grounds of colour, race religion, sex, sexual orientation and disability.

Noise-3.5-Not to play or allow to be played any radio, television, audio equipment or musical instrument so loudly that it causes a nuisance or annoyance to neighbours or can be heard outside the Premises.

Domestic Violence-3.6-Not to use or threaten violence against any other person living in the Premises such that they are forced to leave by reason of the Tenant's violence or fear of such violence.

Pets-3.7-To keep under control any animals at the Premises and to obtain the written consent of the landlord before keeping a dog or any other animal.

Car Repairs-3.8-That no car servicing or car repairs shall be carried out in the roads or accessway or parking spaces or in the forecourt or approaches to the Premises, such as to be a nuisance or annoyance to neighbours.

Paraffin-3.9-Not to use any paraffin or bottled gas heating, lighting or cooking appliances on the Premises nor any appliances which discharge the products of combustion into the interior of the Premises.

Vehicles-3.10-That no commercial vehicle, caravan, boat, or lorry shall be parked in the accessway or parking spaces (regardless of whether this forms part of the Premises) or in the forecourt or approaches to the Premises or the adjoining premises.

Keeping premises clean-3.11-To keep the interior of the Premises in a clean condition. The Tenant agrees to return the property in the same decorative order as at the start of the tenancy taking into account fair wear and tear.

Damage-3.12-To make good any damage caused wilfully or by neglect or carelessness on the part of the Tenant or any member of the Tenant's household or visitor to the Premises including the replacement of any broken glass in windows and repair or replacement of any damaged fittings and installations. If the Tenant fails to make good any damage for which he/she is responsible the landlord may enter the Premises and carry out the work in default and the cost of this work shall be recoverable by the Association from the Tenant.

Reporting Disrepair-3.13-To report to the landlord any disrepair or defect for which the landlord is responsible in the structure or exterior of the Premises or in any installation therein or in the common parts.

Access-3.14-To allow the landlords employees or contractors acting on behalf of the landlord access at all reasonable hours of the daytime to inspect the condition of the Premises or to carry out repairs or other works to the Premises or adjoining property. The landlord will normally give at least 24 hours' notice, but immediate access may be required and shall be given in an emergency.

Assignment-3.15-Not to assign the Tenancy.

Sub-Tenants-3.16-Not to sub-let the whole or part of the Premises.

Ending the Tenancy-3.17-To give the landlord at least [4] weeks notice in writing when the Tenant wishes to end the Tenancy.

Moving Out-3.18-To give the landlord vacant possession and return the keys of the Premises at the end of the Tenancy and to remove all personal possessions and rubbish and leave the Premises and the landlords furniture and fixtures in good lettable condition and repair. The landlord accepts no responsibility for anything left at the Premises by the Tenant at the end of the Tenancy.

4. The Tenant has the following rights:

Right to Occupy-4.1-The Tenant has the right to occupy the Premises without interruption or interference from the landlord for the duration of this Tenancy (except for the obligation contained in this Agreement to give access to the landlords employees or contractors) so long as the Tenant complies with the terms of this Agreement and has proper respect for the rights of other tenants and neighbours.

Security of Tenure-4.2-The Tenant has security of tenure as an assured tenant so long as he/she occupies the Premises as his/her only or principal home. Before the expiry of the fixed term the landlord can only end the Tenancy by obtaining a court order for possession of the Premises on one of the grounds listed in Schedule 2 of the Housing Act 1988. The landlord will only use the following grounds to obtain an order for possession

(i)   --The tenant has not paid rent which is due; (Ground 10)

(ii)   The Tenant has broken, or failed to perform, any of the conditions of this Tenancy; (Ground 12)

162

(iii)   The Tenant or anyone living in the premises has caused damage to, or failed to look after the premises, the building, any of the common parts; (Ground 13)

(iv)   The Tenant or anyone living in the premises has caused serious or persistent nuisance or annoyance to neighbours, or has been responsible for any act of harassment on the grounds of race, colour, religion, sex, sexual orientation, or disability, or has been convicted of using the property for immoral or illegal purposes; (Ground 14) or because of domestic violence (Ground 14A)

(v)   Where the tenancy has devolved under the will or intestacy of the Tenant

(vi)   Suitable alternative accommodation is available to the Tenant

Notice Periods for ending Assured Tenancy-4.3-Before the expiry of the fixed term the landlord agrees that it will not give less than four weeks notice in writing of its intention to seek a possession order except where it is seeking possession on Ground 14 or Ground 14A (whether or not combined with other Grounds) where it shall give such period of notice that it shall decide and that is not less than the statutory minimum notice period

Expiry of Tenancy-4.4-The landlord can only end the Tenancy by giving the Tenant at least two months notice that it requires possession of the Premises and by obtaining a court order for possession. The court will make an order for possession if it is satisfied that the proper notice has been given.

Cessation of Assured Tenancy-4.5-If the Tenancy ceases to be an assured tenancy the landlord may end the Tenancy by giving four weeks' notice in writing which shall be validly served on the Tenant if posted or delivered to the Premises.

(As amended by Section 98 Housing Act 1996)
Section 21 (a or b depending on when served)
Assured Shorthold Tenancy
Notice Requiring Possession

TO:-

  OF:-Address:

  FROM:- (Landlord)

  OF:-

HEREBY GIVE YOU NOTICE THAT POSSESSION IS REQUIRED

by virtue of section 21 Housing Act 1988 of the premises

  -Address:

Which you hold as tenant after the

Signed On behalf of (Landlord):

....

Date: ....

Print Name:

Note

1. If the tenant does not leave the dwelling the landlord must get an order for possession from the court before the tenant can be legally evicted. The landlord cannot apply for such an order before the notice has run out.

2. A tenant who does not know if he has any rights to remain in

possession after a notice runs out or is otherwise unsure of his rights can obtain advice from a solicitor. Help with all or part of the cost of legal advice and assistance may be available under the legal aid scheme. He should also be able to obtain information from a Citizens Advice Bureau, a Housing Aid Centre or a Rent Officer

SCOTLAND

LANDLORDS NOTICE TO TERMINATE

SHORT ASSURED TENANCY

FROM:

LANDLORDS NAME AND
ADDRESS_____

_____

_____

_____

TO:
TENANT_____

_____

_____

_____

DATE_____

PROPERTY_____

_____

_____

_____

The above landlord hereby gives formal notice to the above tenant under section 33 of the Housing (Scotland) Act 1988 of their intention to bring the tenants tenancy to an end and recover possession of the above property currently occupied by the tenant.

In terms of section 33 of the aforementioned Act the tenant must receive at least two months notice of the landlords intention to recover possession. Please therefore take note that you are required to vacate the premises no later than_____

Note: This Notice to terminate and the Notice to Quit overleaf should both be completed and sent to the tenant at least two months before the end of the tenancy.

SCOTLAND

SHORT ASSURED TENANCY NOTICE TO QUIT

NOTI CE OF REMOVAL UNDER SECTION 37 OF THE SHERIFF COURTS (SCOTLAND) ACT 1907

FROM:
LANDLORD_____

_____

_____

TO:
TENANT_____

_____

_____

DATE:_____

PROPERTY_____

_____

The above landlords hereby give notice to the above tenant that the tenant is required to remove from the property at the_____ day of_____ in terms of the lease between landlord and tenant.

The undernoted schedule which is incorporated herein complied with the Assured Tenancies (Notice to Quit Information) (Scotland) Regulations 1988.

Schedule

1. Even after the Notice to Quit has run out, before the tenant can be lawfully evicted, the landlord must get an order or possession from the court.

2. If the landlord issues a Notice to Quit but does not seek to gain possession of the property in question the contractual assured tenancy which has been terminated will be replaced by a Statutory Assured Tenancy. In such circumstances the landlord may propose new terms for the tenancy and may seek an adjustment to the rent at annual intervals thereafter.

3. If a tenant does not know what type of tenancy he has or is otherwise unsure of his rights he can obtain advice from a solicitor. Help with all or part of the cost of legal advice and assistance can be available under the legal aid legislation. A tenant can also seek help from a Citizens Advice Bureau or Housing Advisory centre.

ENGLAND AND WALES AND SCOTLAND HOUSEHOLD INVENTORY

Re: (The Property)_____

Living room				
No	Item	Condition	In	Out
1	Armchair	Fair		(condition when leaving)
Etc Etc				
Kitchen				
Bathroom				

Hall				
Bedroom (1-2-3)				
Garden				
Other